Schindler House

Schindler House

Kathryn Smith

New photography by Grant Mudford

To Randy
–Kathryn

To R. M. S.
–Grant

Reprinted with permission 2010 by

Hennessey + Ingalls
214 Wilshire Boulevard
Santa Monica CA 90401

www.hennesseyingalls.com

ISBN: 978-0-940512-50-4
California Architecture and Architects, No. 31

First published 2001 by Harry N. Abrams

Library of Congress Cataloging-in-Publication Data

Smith, Kathryn, 1945-
Schindler House / Kathryn Smith ; new photography by Grant Mudford.
    p. cm.
Originally published: New York : Harry N. Abrams, 2001.
Includes bibliographical references and index.
ISBN 978-0-940512-50-4
1. Schindler House (Los Angeles, Calif.) 2. Schindler, R. M. (Rudolph M.), 1887-1953–
Criticism and interpretation. 3. Schindler, R. M. (Rudolph M.), 1887-1953–Homes and
haunts–California–Los Angeles. 4. Modern movement (Architecture)–California–Los
Angeles. 5. Wright, Frank Lloyd, 1867-1959–Influence. 6. Los Angeles (Calif.)–
Buildings, structures, etc. I. Mudford, Grant, 1944- II. Title.

NA7238.L6S633 2010
728.092–dc22
                              2009050876

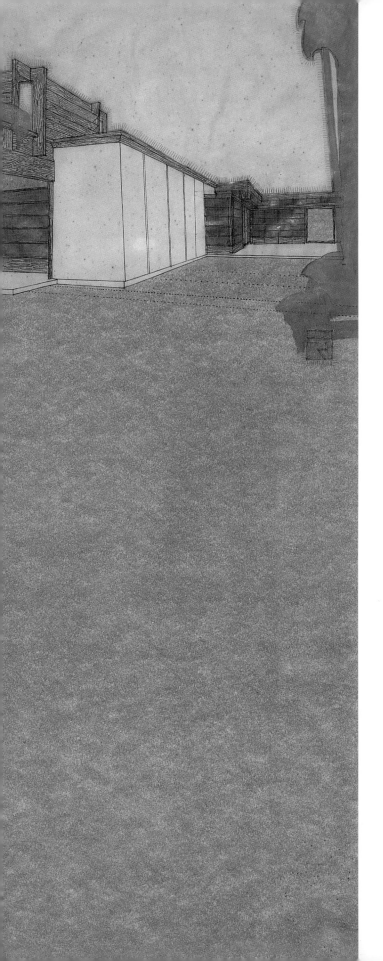

Contents

7   Schindler House, 1921–22 *Kathryn Smith*

44 Photograph Portfolio *Grant Mudford*

80 Appendix A, R. M. Schindler, Letter to Mr. and
    Mrs. Edmund J. Gibling, November 26, 1921

81 Appendix B, R. M. Schindler, "A Cooperative
    Dwelling," *T-Square*, February 1932

83 Selected Bibliography

84 Acknowledgments *Kathryn Smith*

86 Index

88 Photograph Credits

Schindler House, 1921–22 Kathryn Smith

The Schindler House was designed in November 1921 by R. M. Schindler for two couples – Schindler and his wife, Sophie Pauline Gibling, and Clyde and Marian Chace – in West Hollywood, California. When it was completed, in June 1922, it looked completely different from any other house in the neighborhood. In fact, it looked completely different from any other house in the United States. But the importance of the house is greater than an issue of style: it was no less than the first modern house to be built in the world.[1] Designed, as the English historian and critic Reyner Banham wrote, "as if there had never been houses before,"[2] the Schindler House was the first executed realization of a new kind of residential architecture for the modern world.[3] In every one of its key elements – its program, its plan, its materials, its construction system, and especially, in its spatial relationships – it broke decisively with tradition. As a result, "the Schindler House comes disturbingly near to being a totally new beginning,"[4] declared Banham. The idea of starting over with a completely fresh slate was a preoccupation of modern architects. But how did this happen so far away from the international centers of intellectual ferment and artistic revolt – Paris, Berlin, and Moscow? It was a question of opportunity.

Vienna, Chicago, and Wright

Rudolph Michael Schindler was a first-generation architect of the twentieth century. He was born in Vienna on September 10, 1887, the same year as Le Corbusier. Schindler's formative years took place against the backdrop of fin-de-siècle Vienna, a cosmopolitan European capital noted for its philosophic debate and artistic experimentation. Schindler came of age in the city of Sigmund Freud and Ludwig Wittgenstein, Arnold Schönberg and Gustav Klimt, Otto Wagner and Adolph Loos.

Schindler began his study of architecture at the Imperial Technical University, where he was enrolled from 1906 to 1911. In 1910 he entered the Academy of Fine Arts and joined Wagner's prestigious studio, where he spent three academic years. In addition to his formal studies, Schindler also attended lectures given by Loos at what Loos called his "Bauschule," his informal architectural school. It was at this time that he met Richard Neutra, five years his junior, who was still at the Technical University. Between 1911 and 1914 Schindler obtained practical experience at the firm of Mayr and Mayer. As a result of this progressive education and training, at an early date he rejected academic architecture in favor of an interest in industrial materials and methods, a simplification of form, and an awareness of architecture as the manipulation of space.

Entrance to Chace studios, with sleeping basket above

The pivotal moment in Schindler's life occurred in 1914 when, at the urging of Loos, who had himself spent several years in the United States in the 1890s, he left Europe to sail for America. In late 1913 Schindler had answered an advertisement for a position at the Chicago firm of Ottenheimer, Stern, and Reichert. By February 1914 the details of Schindler's employment were worked out in correspondence with William Reichert. The offer called for a term of three months, with an option, if both parties were satisfied, to stay an additional six months.[5] Schindler's boat, the *Kaiserin Auguste Victoria*, docked in New York on March 8, 1914, just five months before the outbreak of World War I. "New York, after the long days on the plane of water," Schindler recalled, "rose out of the bottom of the bay as an adventure – the city."[6] By March 12 he was at his drafting board in Chicago at work on the National Home of the B.P.O. Elks.

Schindler's attitude toward his new job is evident in a letter he wrote to Frank Lloyd Wright in November 1914. "During the summer I tried several times without success to meet you," he confided, "– and hope now this letter may be a better mean to reach my aim." He admitted that he could not "help to feel unhappy in an average American office," adding, "this feeling is growing from day to day and my only hope is to come in touch with you." He closed by revealing, perhaps, the true reason he chose Chicago as the place to seek his American prospects: "So I ask if you could admit me to your office, or give me an opportunity to study your finished works at a closer range or suggest any other way of getting some breaths of a better archect. atmosphere."[7]

Construction of Elks Club, Chicago, 1916. Schindler supervised the erection of this steel-frame building. Photograph by R. M. Schindler

It was with good reason that Schindler had come to America to seek out Wright. His work was well known in European architectural circles by 1914. Wright had been practicing as an independent architect for just over twenty years, having struck out on his own in 1893 after an apprenticeship with Adler and Sullivan, a firm known for their high-rise commercial buildings. By 1900 he had created the Prairie House, a residential type that appealed to a progressive segment of Chicago's middle class because it represented a practical, new way of life – full of "light, air, and prospect"[8] – in contrast to the claustrophobic, cluttered rooms of the Victorian house. The spatial innovation of the plan – with the public rooms open to each other on the diagonal, creating a fluid arrangement – was made feasible by the invention of mechanical heating systems. Wright seized this opportunity to eliminate the compartmentalization of the Victorian house – the boxes within a box – and replaced it with dynamic movement as walls began to define, rather than enclose, space. While the Prairie House demonstrated Wright's talent with the single-family dwelling, the commissions he received to design public buildings between 1902 and 1908 enabled him to usher in a rigorous abstraction attuned to the spirit of the industrial age. The solid rectangular block of the Larkin Administration Building in Buffalo, New York (1902–6), and the cubic severity of Unity Temple in Oak Park, Illinois (1905–8), represented a search for a monumental architectural language for the twentieth century.

In 1910 Ernst Wasmuth in Berlin published Wright's work of these years as a deluxe, elephant portfolio, designed under the architect's personal supervision. Its dissemination in Europe in the years preceding the war had a serious impact on the first generation of modern architects; yet Schindler was the first European architect who had seen the Wasmuth portfolio to emigrate to America and approach Wright for work in his studio. Schindler's eagerness to join Wright is clear by the date of his letter – November 1914 – exactly eight months after his arrival in Chicago and, according to his correspondence with Ottenheimer, Stern, and Reichert, just one month before the end of his original term of employment.

Although it was the Prairie Houses, which he had studied in the Wasmuth portfolio, that brought Schindler to Wright, Wright had moved on and was exploring new ground. By 1911 he had separated from his wife and children in Oak Park and built Taliesin, a house and studio in the countryside of Wisconsin, a day's train trip from Chicago. In the first decade at Taliesin, Wright's work load diminished and his studio staff was reduced to a few trusted assistants. The possibility of larger commissions – in particular, a new hotel for Tokyo, Japan – loomed in the future, but in 1914 the best Wright could offer Schindler was a letter of introduction to one of his Prairie House clients.[9]

Another three years elapsed before Schindler was able to realize his ambition of working with Wright. While he was waiting, he continued at Ottenheimer, Stern, and Reichert. In 1915 Schindler went on a vacation to California, stopping in New Mexico and Arizona along the way. His growing disillusionment with the commercial

Schindler in Taos, New Mexico, 1915

architecture of Chicago was in stark contrast to his enthusiasm for the pueblos of Taos, New Mexico. "The few skyscrapers which were thrust upward by the gigantic vitality of the infinitely fertile prairies have nothing human about them," Schindler wrote to his friend Neutra. "The only buildings which testify to the deep feeling for the soil on which they stand are the sun-baked adobe buildings of the first immigrants and their successors – Spanish and Mexican – in the southwestern part of the country," he concluded.[10]

Schindler wanted to return to Europe, but two things stopped him. First, correspondence with friends at home painted a desperate picture of the economic and social conditions wrought by the war. "Everywhere is extreme squalidness," Neutra wrote, "and it may be ten years before we see the first seeds of change sprouting. If I could just get over there [to America] – how much I would like that!"[11] Second was the possibility of working with Wright, and by late 1917 they were able to reach an agreement. The building committee of the Buena Shore Club had hired Schindler to supervise construction of its clubhouse, which he had designed as an

Pueblo, Taos, New Mexico, 1915. This site was the highlight of Schindler's first trip across the Southwest. Photograph by R. M. Schindler

Chicago, view toward Michigan Avenue with the Art Institute on the right, 1916. Frank Lloyd Wright's office was located in the Monroe Building, opposite the Art Institute. Photograph by R. M. Schindler

employee of Ottenheimer, Stern, and Reichert. As a result, Schindler left the firm on November 1 to spend the last months of the year completing the largest building he would ever design in his career. Wright invited him to use his Chicago office in the Monroe Building while he was away on a trip and, when the Buena Shore Club was completed, to join him at Taliesin in February to begin producing the working drawings for his new commission, the Imperial Hotel in Tokyo.[12]

When Schindler went to work for Wright he went prepared. In addition to the knowledge he had acquired through his study of the Wasmuth portfolio, he had toured Wright's buildings throughout Chicago with a camera in hand. "He is the first architect – the first who truly accomplishes what I was looking for and defended in the Wagner School," Schindler professed; "his art is spatial art in the true sense of the word and has completely shed the characteristics of sculpture which all architecture of the past possessed. The room is not a box – the walls have disappeared and free nature flows through his houses as in a forest. He is a complete and perfect master of any material – and modern machine techniques are at the base of his form-making."[13]

In those first few months of 1918 Schindler could never have predicted what an unusual role he would ultimately play in Wright's studio. Wright approached the job in Tokyo with his usual optimistic bravado; he declared that it would take two years of his time with only a few months spent in Japan. Instead the mammoth project kept him there for the better part of the next four years, with only annual short trips back home. Construction dragged on until 1922, and when he left Tokyo for good that year, the hotel still was not completed. While in Tokyo, Wright needed a reliable and knowledgeable employee in Chicago to oversee his affairs: to coordinate with consulting American engineers, to order and ship building supplies and equipment to Japan, to field new clients, and, if necessary, to design and execute new commissions. The latter was a circumstance that was unprecedented in Wright's career, and he was obviously uncomfortable with it. Yet his real need for income motivated him in 1919 to write Schindler from Tokyo:

Frank Lloyd Wright at Taliesin,
Spring Green, Wisconsin, 1924

Wright's staff at the entrance to
the studio at Taliesin, 1918. From
left to right, William E. Smith,
Schindler, Arato Endo, Goichi
Fujikura, and Julius Floto. Floto
was the consulting structural
engineer on the Imperial Hotel;
the other four were draftsmen

The drafting room at Taliesin,
1918. Drawings for the Imperial
Hotel can be seen on the boards.
Photograph by R. M. Schindler

It seems to me to hope, Rudolph, that you are not going to turn out to be the same kind of damn fool that I have been pestered with all these years. Regarding the prospective clients – "Schindler" is keeping my office and my work for me in my absence. He has no identity as "Schindler" with clients who want "Wright" therefore – has he? I really do not know quite what a "Schindler" would look like. You know much better what a "Wright" would look like and be like and as the clients came to get it – the natural thing would be it would seem to lay it out as nearly as you can as I would do it and send it here for straightening. This might give a result that would not mar your conscience beyond repair and something good still might result and the clients in no way cheated. Nicht Wahr? This seems quite obvious enough and I think you can be trusted to do it quite well and need not be squeamish even if a little Schindler is thrown in for good measure. "Wright" is supposed to have left his work with someone competent to represent him in his absence.[14]

As a result of Wright's unusual situation, Schindler took over more responsibilities than were customary, including the design of several jobs, most of which were minor. However, in early 1919 a former Prairie House client, Thomas P. Hardy, brought into the office a larger commission for a residential development in Racine, Wisconsin. All evidence points conclusively to Schindler as the designer for what was labeled a "Workingman's Colony of Concrete Monolith Houses," a project to build eighteen houses on a site bordering the Root River.[15] In July 1919 Schindler drew a preliminary first- and second-floor plan and a perspective. These drawings were followed in the same month by five sheets of working drawings, a site plan, and a perspective of the overall development.

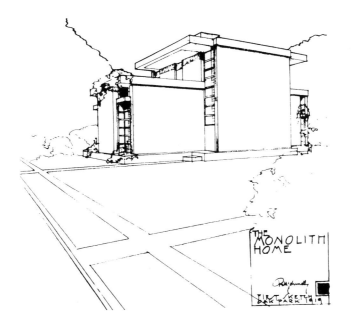

R. M. Schindler for Frank Lloyd Wright, The Monolith Home, Racine, Wisconsin, presentation drawing, 1919

The Monolith Home, as it was eventually titled, was based on the theme of using one material, cast concrete, throughout the exterior and interior – for floors, walls, and roof. The drawings show a building on a two-foot square grid, wholly composed of solid and transparent planes. With one exception – in the storage room – no two walls are joined at right angles to enclose a corner. In the slots between the slabs, strips of transparent glass extended from floor to ceiling – and, in some areas, the full two stories – in an unbroken rhythm of units, virtually erasing the distinction between doors and windows. To open the living room on the diagonal, Schindler butted two vertical strips of glass together to create an inverted corner window.

Although inspired by Wright's earlier work both formally and structurally, Schindler's scheme went an important step further in its degree of abstraction and its uncompromising use of unfinished concrete. The consequences were threefold: structurally, the materials declared their industrial origins and implied methods of mass production; socially, the low-cost, minimal dwelling was directed at the worker; spatially, outside and inside interpenetrated fluidly through the vertical slots of glass, although the interior was compartmentalized to accommodate the program. In these essential respects the Monolith Home surpassed the contemporary work of Ludwig Mies van der Rohe, Walter Gropius, and Gerrit Rietveld in its modernism. Only Le Corbusier's Monol House, also of 1919 (which predated the Citrohan House by a year), exhibited the same rationalist vigor and progressive social vision. The Monolith Home was nothing short of an industrialized product, stripped of classical ornament and traditional decoration, yet it was elevated to the status of art by its balanced proportion and complex spatial relationships. The house was a European challenge to the American status quo. It was unfortunately never built.

Wright received one other major commission while Schindler worked in his studio. It was for the oil heiress Aline Barnsdall, who wanted to build a theater community on Olive Hill in Hollywood, California, with a house for herself as the centerpiece. Based in various locations, Schindler worked on plans and drawings for Barnsdall's house, which later was called "Hollyhock House," and on the Imperial Hotel. While Wright was in Tokyo, Schindler stayed in a converted apartment in Wright's Oak Park studio and conducted business in the downtown Chicago office on Michigan Avenue. When Wright was back in the Midwest, Schindler and Wright's other assistant, William E. Smith, moved up to Taliesin.

In the spring of 1919, during one of Wright's prolonged absences in Japan and while Schindler was living in Oak Park, Schindler met Sophie Pauline Gibling (b. Minneapolis, March 19, 1893; d. Los Angeles, May 4, 1977) at the American premiere of Prokofiev's *Scythian Suite*. After graduating from Smith College, Pauline had begun teaching music at Jane Addams's Hull House in Chicago and at a school in the northern suburb of Ravinia. Her insatiable curiosity, along with her intensity regarding progressive social, political, and artistic movements, must have proven immediately attractive to Schindler. Despite the intellectual disdain they shared concerning traditional institutions, Pauline and Schindler were married on August 29, 1919, agreeing that they

The entrance to Taliesin, 1918.
Photograph by R. M. Schindler

The court at Taliesin, 1918. From
left to right are the studio, the
loggia, and Wright's living quarters.
Photograph by R. M. Schindler

The living room at Taliesin, 1918,
with many pieces from Wright's
Asian art collection. Photograph
by R. M. Schindler

Pauline Schindler at Taliesin, 1920.
Photograph by R. M. Schindler

Schindler at Taliesin, 1920

would maintain their independence yet share their life as a couple. They resided at Wright's Oak Park studio until April 1920, when they moved to a rented room. On Wright's return in July, he invited them to Taliesin.

The Schindlers were deeply moved by Taliesin, especially its organization as an artist's studio where buildings and landscape were in harmony and where the simplicity of farm life heightened the sophisticated appreciation of the arts. Pauline could barely contain her enthusiasm as she explained to her parents, "There are such strong contrasts – such primitive simplicity of life beside things of the highest possible finish and texture. After I have been churning butter, perhaps, or talked for a while with a lonely horse in a pasture, I come back into the studio and look for a while at the model of the Los Angeles buildings. Like going from folk-song to Schönberg or Debussy."[16] Seduced by the atmosphere at Taliesin, the Schindlers began to talk of building their own studio someday.

Schindler's choice of Los Angeles as a place to settle in 1920 was really accidental. Just after Thanksgiving, Wright sent him there to supervise the construction of Hollyhock House and the adjoining structures for Barnsdall, with the hint of a trip to Japan in the future. Schindler and his wife traveled to Los Angeles by train, sightseeing across the Southwest. The trip to Tokyo eventually fell through, but Schindler was attracted to Los Angeles's climate and bountiful landscape of orchards, canyons, and hills.

By the time he arrived in Hollywood, Schindler had completed two years with Wright and was beginning to realize that the work was not what he had expected from his study of the Wasmuth portfolio. In his buildings from 1914 onward, Wright was increasingly interested in modern construction and materials (especially reinforced concrete) and in organizing the building process as an ordered system (analogous to machine manufacture), but he was also deepening his awareness of preindustrial Japanese, pre-Columbian, and Native American cultures. Wright was after more than stylistic parallels; he was trying to recapture the spirit of a direct connection to nature. More

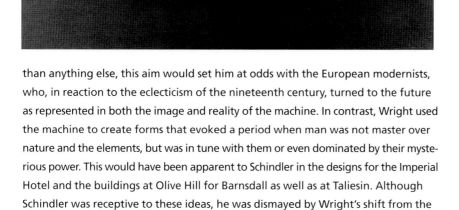

Frank Lloyd Wright, Hollyhock House, Hollywood, front elevation, 1920–21

than anything else, this aim would set him at odds with the European modernists, who, in reaction to the eclecticism of the nineteenth century, turned to the future as represented in both the image and reality of the machine. In contrast, Wright used the machine to create forms that evoked a period when man was not master over nature and the elements, but was in tune with them or even dominated by their mysterious power. This would have been apparent to Schindler in the designs for the Imperial Hotel and the buildings at Olive Hill for Barnsdall as well as at Taliesin. Although Schindler was receptive to these ideas, he was dismayed by Wright's shift from the abstract planar compositions of the Oak Park years to a more monumental architecture of sculptural weight and ornamental presence, perceiving it as retrogression.

This disappointment was balanced by Schindler's deepening acquaintance with and admiration for Los Angeles architect Irving Gill, who was seventeen years his senior. Much later Schindler recalled, "I came [to Los Angeles] to take charge of some buildings on Olive Hill that were designed in Frank Lloyd Wright's Chicago office. Although in a very interesting and personal language, they clung to the classical Greek vocabulary (base, shaft, cornice), at the same time trying to give themselves local roots by the introduction of Mayan motifs." He added, "When I arrived here

Irving Gill, La Jolla Woman's Club, La Jolla, California, 1913. The club was built using the tilt-slab construction method

in 1921, the only local architect who had made any consistent effort to break with tradition and the fashionable 'Spanish Style' was Mr. Irving Gill, who tried to drop all meaningless style forms and reduce the building to a simple mass form."[17]

Gill became more influential to Schindler when Clyde and Marian Chace moved to Los Angeles in the summer of 1921. Marian Da Camara Chace (b. Florida, August 1, 1892; d. California, November 17, 1978) and Pauline had become close friends while attending Smith College and later living together in Ravinia. Clyde Burgess Chace (b. Kansas City, Missouri, July 2, 1891; d. California, December 21, 1991), trained as an engineer, came at the Schindlers' suggestion to do drafting, estimating, and contracting for Gill; by September the couple had rented a house at the beach with him. Gill's experiments with concrete were of particular interest to Schindler, especially his tilt-slab method of constructing walls by pouring concrete into molds and tilting the prefabricated sections into place after they cured.[18] Through Chace's association with Gill, Schindler would later have access to Gill's technical expertise and even his equipment.

In October 1921, at the conclusion of the Barnsdall job, the Schindlers spent several weeks camping at Yosemite National Park. They decided that Schindler would open his architectural practice in Los Angeles and that they would build their own studio-residence, which they had dreamed of since living at Taliesin. The spirit that they felt at Yosemite – removed from the monotony and pressures of day-to-day responsibilities – was to affect the planning of their own house.

Site, Design, and Construction

The Schindlers had discussed building with the Chaces before their trip to Yosemite, but on November 11, 1921, they met to plan in earnest. To save costs Schindler and Chace agreed to work together as architect and builder, respectively. By November 21 they were surveying the lot, a generous 100 x 200-foot property on tree-lined

Kings Road. Could it have been a coincidence that the land Schindler chose was only one block from Gill's cast-concrete Dodge House of 1914–16 (and notably, a building reminiscent of Loos's Steiner House of 1910)?[19]

We can only speculate on the various factors that contributed to the genesis of Schindler's plan for a modern house for the twentieth century. The Monolith Home had laid out his intentions regarding materials, construction systems, and a social vision; it was an early experiment. Although he and Pauline had undoubtedly discussed ideas for their own studio off and on since they left Taliesin, especially during their vacation at Yosemite, there are no surviving conceptual sketches or notes that document their conversations. The fact that Schindler and Pauline, both before and during their marriage, kept current with progressive ideas about modern life circulating between Europe and America provided an underlying intellectual context. Through avant-garde magazines such as *The Little Review* and friends they had made in Chicago and Los Angeles, they followed emerging movements in the arts, whether music, dance, painting, or photography; they debated the latest theories about social reform, education, and psychoanalysis; and they adopted, not always consistently, philosophies that promoted healthy diet, exercise, and even the wearing of soft, unstructured clothing.

It is doubtful that the Chaces were the source for the innovations in the program, although Marian would have been sympathetic since she and Pauline had debated theories of ideal societies while in college. Surviving correspondence reveals that

Aerial view of Beverly Hills and West Hollywood, February 11, 1922

while Pauline ferociously promoted and defended the revolutionary nature of the house in letters to her mother, she was simultaneously making plans to add her own traditional touches, such as hooked rugs and painted walls.

The document that provides the clearest idea of Schindler's intentions in his first independent building is a letter he wrote to his wife's parents, dated November 26, 1921, accompanying a request for a loan (see Appendix A). That the design was finalized within a period of only two weeks immediately following his return from the mountains reveals how vividly Schindler's recent idyllic interlude in the American wilderness affected him. He wrote, "The basic idea was to give each person his own room – instead of the usual distribution – and to do most of the cooking right on the table – making it more a social 'campfire' affair, than the disagreeable burden to one member of the family."[20]

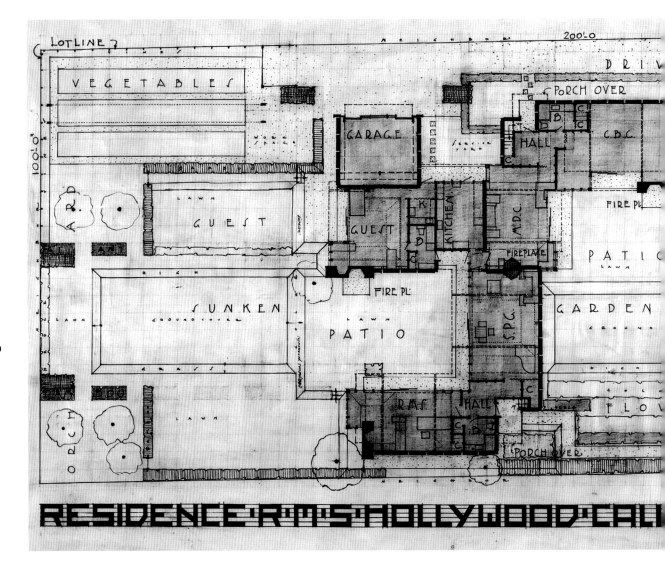

The concept of separate studios represented Schindler's interpretation of the family as a group of independent individuals with common goals; it implied that each member was an artist whose life was a confident expression of creativity. He eliminated conventional kitchens for each couple (and thus the drudgery of the housewife's routine), choosing instead to have a common kitchen and to bring utilities into the wall beside the fireplaces, so that cooking and cleanup could take place informally in the studios. "The rooms are large studiorooms," Schindler explained, "with concrete walls on three sides, the front open (glass) to the out-doors – a real California scheme."[21] With the memory of his shelter at Yosemite still vivid in his mind, he sought to impart to his own house the same freedom and celebration of life he had experienced in nature – the psychology of a perpetual vacation where the irritations of the workaday world could be evaded.

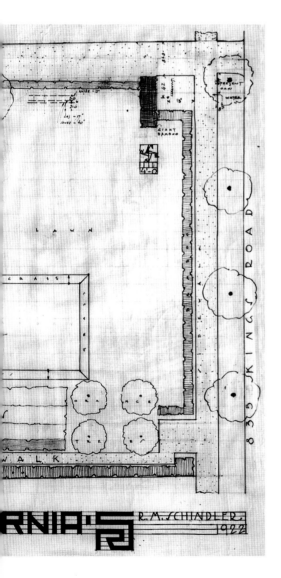

Ground floor plan, 1922. In the upper margin (not visible in this photo) Schindler calculated the square footage: RMS, 1040; CBC, 1000; Guest, 410; Kitchen, 210; Garage, 300 = 2960 square feet + porches, 450

Irving Gill, Dodge House, West Hollywood, 1914–16 (demolished 1968)

Wall and roof construction, ca. April 6–24, 1922

Building the redwood framing and roof on the Clyde Chace studio, ca. April 24–May 1, 1922

Chronology of construction, 1922

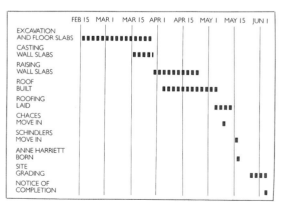

	FEB 15	MAR 1	MAR 15	APR 1	APR 15	MAY 1	MAY 15	JUN 1
EXCAVATION AND FLOOR SLABS	■■■■■■■■■■■							
CASTING WALL SLABS			■■■■					
RAISING WALL SLABS				■■■■■■■■				
ROOF BUILT				■■■■■■■■■■				
ROOFING LAID						■■■		
CHACES MOVE IN						■		
SCHINDLERS MOVE IN							■	
ANNE HARRIETT BORN							■	
SITE GRADING								■■ ■
NOTICE OF COMPLETION								■

From left to right, guest studio
and Schindler studios, summer
1922. Note the projecting glass
bay on R. M. Schindler's studio,
at right

Pauline Schindler studio, 1929

Just as construction was to commence, the ideal gave way to reality when, by the end of January 1922, both Marian Chace and Pauline Schindler announced that they were pregnant, the former to deliver in May and the latter in August. Since the original design did not address the possibility of children, a suggestion that two nurseries be added as part of each woman's studio was introduced by mid-February. However, when the Chace nursery was designed, probably during construction in April, it was created by incorporating it within the Clyde Chace studio. The Schindler nursery was never built; instead, the following year a sunroom was added to the Schindler "sleeping basket," one of two open-air porches on the roof that were just large enough to contain a bed.

On February 13 Schindler celebrated the impending groundbreaking by executing a dramatic presentation drawing in black and gold. He had secured a first mortgage of $5000 from a bank and a second mortgage of $2000 from the Giblings. As of February 15 excavation and pouring of the floor slabs was under way. Chace borrowed some concrete equipment from Gill (that had been used in his Horatio West Courts) and by the middle of March the tilt-up slab walls were being fabricated. By March 19 all the walls had been cast except for those of Pauline's and Schindler's studios, which were finished the following week. Between March 28 and April 24 the walls were raised in place, starting with the garage; the roofing then commenced. Schindler was working days on his commissions and nights at the Kings Road site. On April 20 he wrote of the house to his wife in El Centro, where she had accepted a three-month teaching job, "I like it – we shall not have to be grown ups in there – it reaches only to our shoulders – and will play with us."[22]

The Schindler-Gibling family in the Schindler court, summer 1923. From left to right, R. M. Schindler, Pauline Schindler, parents Sophie and Edmund Gibling (holding Mark Schindler), and sister Dorothy Gibling

Schindler kept a ledger of his estimates of the costs of the project and the monetary value of both owners' professional services. The list is as follows: $2750 for the lot, $7000 for construction (labor and materials), $500 for the architect's supervision, $1000 for the contractor's profit, $800 for the architect's fee, and $500 for the owner's labor, for a total of $12,550.[23] By the beginning of May 1922 the budget had been exhausted, leaving nothing for furniture, landscaping, or the sleeping baskets, yet Schindler was pleased.[24] "Architecturally I am satisfied – it is a thoroughbred – and will either attract people – or repulse them – my fate is settled – one way or other," he wrote to the Giblings. "Of course, it will take a couple of years, until the planting will furnish the proper and indispensable setting."[25]

A Cooperative Dwelling

The period between the summers of 1922 and 1924, when the Chaces left Kings Road, were difficult years for both young couples, defined by the arrival of babies, medical and financial problems, and a struggle to establish a new kind of architecture in an unfamiliar setting. The Schindlers' lives had changed dramatically since their carefree vacation at Yosemite, and their marriage began to suffer because of it.

From May through July 1922 the Schindlers and Chaces were camping out at Kings Road.[26] Although the gas and electricity were eventually turned on, they had no furniture except beds, a few low stools, and a piano in Pauline's studio. The need for comfortable surroundings became more urgent when Marian gave birth – to a daughter, Ann Harriett – on May 21. Schindler and Chace worked until late at night installing magnesite counters and tubs in the bathrooms and putting up shelves. And even though Schindler had dictated "no paint," the two old college friends, known to each other as "Gibbi" (Pauline) and "Kimmie" (Marian), could not be restrained from staining some of the Insulite panels green-gold.

On July 20 the Schindlers' son, Mark, was born prematurely. For the remainder of the year the two women were devoted to the care of their infants and spent little time at work on the property. The cooperative household worked smoothly, with Gibbi and Kimmie often watching over each other's child. Schindler and Chace made furniture for the guest studio to accommodate its first occupant, Pauline's sister, Dorothy Gibling.

During this time Schindler and Chace were at work (as architect and builder, respectively) on a house in the desert for Paul Popenoe and then, in 1923, on the Pueblo Ribera Courts in La Jolla. Both structures were built using concrete prefabrication techniques, which Schindler called "slab-tilt" (which he employed on the Schindler House) and "slab-cast," the Popenoe House utilizing the former method and the Pueblo Ribera Courts the latter.[27] While they were out of town on jobs, other members of the Kings Road household continued to make furniture, install shelves and tables, and add to the existing building and gardens. And by the middle of summer 1923, the Schindler sleeping basket was built.[28]

Despite the excitement of seeing works of modern architecture come to fruition, little income trickled in between Schindler and Chace. Finances were further aggravated by expensive emergencies: Pauline was operated on for a perforated ulcer in January 1923; Chace had an operation in January 1924; and Marian gave birth to a son, Robert, in April 1924. Although there were shortages of money, the Kings Road house was very active with social life, especially after Wright arrived in January 1923 in Los Angeles, to move his practice there. He brought with him an interesting group of young architects, which included Kameki and Nobu Tsuchiura, Werner and Sylva Moser, and William E. Smith. All spent time visiting and even living at Kings Road, where they joined the Schindlers' widening circle of friends in the arts and politics.

In July 1924 the Chaces left Kings Road to move to Florida,[29] having accepted an offer to join Marian's family business. Their departure, however, coincided with Schindler's first meeting in Chicago with his old friend Neutra, newly arrived from war-torn Europe.[30]

Architectural Partnership

Richard Neutra (b. Vienna, April 8, 1892; d. Wuppertal, Germany, April 16, 1970), his wife, Dione (b. Switzerland, April 14, 1901; d. Los Angeles, September 1, 1990), and their son, Frank, arrived at the Kings Road house in March 1925, after a few months' stay at Taliesin. They lived first in the guest studio, then moved into the Chace studios after they were vacated by tenants who had rented them since the Chaces' departure. Neutra at once set in motion plans to establish himself as an architect, giving public lectures, teaching, writing books, entering competitions,

26

Dione Neutra at the entrance to the Chace sleeping basket, 1925

and obtaining his architectural license. Dione supported his efforts by taking care of the household and the children (a second son, Dion, was born in October 1926).

During these years Schindler's practice grew in importance, his marriage deteriorated irrevocably, and in 1926 he joined in partnership with Neutra (under the name The Architectural Group for Industry and Commerce), which ultimately revealed their aesthetic and temperamental differences to be greater than their common interests. After several years of real struggle and severe financial strain, Schindler was attracting more substantial and satisfying jobs. In the fall of 1925 he was asked by Phillip and Leah Lovell to design several houses for them. By the following spring Schindler was at work on a mountain cottage, a ranch house, and a beach house for the couple, with the promise of a large city residence for the next year. The connection with the Lovells was deepened by a friendship between Pauline Schindler and Leah Lovell, who together had started a school called the Children's Workshop in the fall of 1925. With this work and the prospect of a new house for Barnsdall in Palos Verdes, Schindler had his biggest commissions since leaving Wright.

The arrival of the Neutra family both continued the communal spirit of the Schindler House and transformed its character. Despite Pauline's moods and physical problems, her intellectual intensity attracted people in the arts and social reform. During this period the house was often alive with parties; groups of eight or eighty would gather for music and conversation. The openness of the plan facilitated gatherings of different sizes. Sometimes, when more than a hundred guests were expected, the interior partitions filled with Insulite – conceived as non-load-bearing frames – were removed.

Dione Neutra and her sister, Doris Niedermann, in the Marian Chace studio, ca. 1926–28

Doris Niedermann and Dione Neutra in the Marian Chace studio, ca. 1926–28

During these years at the Kings Road studios Schindler and Neutra produced some of their generation's most significant contributions to modern architecture, including Schindler's Lovell Beach House at Newport Beach (1925–26), their joint competition entry for the League of Nations Building (1926), and Neutra's Lovell "Health" House in Los Angeles (1928–29). Neutra also wrote and published two important books, *Wie Baut Amerika?* (1927) and *Amerika* (1930).

Despite these accomplishments, or perhaps because of them, relationships continued to deteriorate at Kings Road. Fundamental differences and strongly held opinions probably had more to do with the growing estrangements than with specific incidents, which were merely excuses to terminate what had ended long before. In August 1927 Pauline moved out of the house with Mark. That year Schindler's name was removed from the drawings of the League of Nations Building on exhibit in Europe, and the commission for the Lovell "Health" House (the city residence) was awarded to Neutra alone. The Neutras stayed at Kings Road until the middle of 1930, when they left on an extended trip out of the country. On returning to Los Angeles they moved elsewhere and eventually built their own house in Silverlake. Schindler and Neutra continued to lecture together, teaching a course on modern architecture in the summer of 1931, but the closeness and comradeship they once had felt was gone.

While the Schindlers and Neutras still occupied the Kings Road house together, modern art dealer and collector Galka Scheyer and dancer John Bovingdon were introduced into their circle. Scheyer, the American representative of the Blue Four (the painters Vasily Kandinsky, Alexei Jawlensky, Paul Klee, and Lyonel Feininger), had rented the guest studio during the summer of 1927 and returned to live in the Chace studios between 1931 and 1933. She was so impressed by Schindler's talent that she gave him the nickname "Five," in obvious reference to the Blue Four.

28

Dion and Dione Neutra (seated), Richard Neutra, and Schindler in the Schindler court, 1928

Galka Scheyer in the Clyde
Chace studio, 1931–33

Bovingdon had returned from Java and Bali full of enthusiasm for the native dance there. He lived at various times in both the guest studio and the Chace studios. He is remembered for the haunting dances he performed in the gardens during large parties, in which he and his bare-breasted female partner acted out symbolic rituals from Bali.

The studios continued to house various creative people in the following decades. Guests and tenants included the novelist Theodore Dreiser, the photographer Edward Weston, and the composer John Cage, along with numerous lesser-known artists and political activists.

By the end of the 1920s all of the primary residents of the house had departed except Schindler, who stayed until his death at age sixty-five. From his studio at 835 North Kings Road, he worked for the rest of his career, producing more than 150 projects in southern California, including such major buildings as the Lovell Beach House, Wolfe House (1928), Elliot House (1930), Oliver House (1933), Rodakiewicz House (1937), and Tischler House (1949–50). Although Schindler's practice consisted mainly of single-family dwellings, he built several larger commissions, such as the Sachs (1926) and Laurelwood Apartments (1948) and the Bethlehem Baptist Church (1944). He died in Los Angeles on August 22, 1953.

In the late 1930s Pauline Schindler returned to the Kings Road house, where she lived, separate from her former husband, in the Chace studios. During these years Mark was often away at boarding school. After Schindler's death and until her own, nearly twenty-four years later, Pauline continued to be engaged in progressive politics and was kept busy entertaining visitors from America and abroad who came to see the Schindler House.

Program, Materials, Plan, Building System, and Space

With the Kings Road house, his first independent building, Schindler took a decisive step away from Wright in favor of austere abstraction, inventive construction techniques, and an audacious interpretation of housing for the modern era. So revolutionary was the program that Schindler dispensed with conventional room types: there is no living room, dining room, or bedroom in the house. The plan called for four studios connected to a utility room,[31] which was neither kitchen, laundry, sewing room, nor storage, but was meant to serve the functions of all four; a separate guest studio with its own bath and kitchen; and a two-car garage. Each studio was designated for one member of the household, identified on the plan by his or her initials: RMS (R. M. Schindler), SPG (Sophie Pauline Gibling Schindler), MDC (Marian Da Camara Chace), and CBC (Clyde Burgess Chace).[32] For sleeping he provided the sleeping baskets. Architecturally they consisted of a canopy and beams that met four posts at mitred corners (a canvas sling on two sides gave protection from the rain). Visually, they were planes supported on spider legs.

Clearly, the idea of studios had a precedent: Wright's Taliesin. Yet his country retreat consisted of three distinct parts: the residence (with conventional room types), the architectural studio, and the farm wing. Schindler's philosophy was less conventional; not only did he dispense with traditional room arrangement, but he designed each studio as a universal space. In other words, it existed as a void and derived its meaning from the furniture arrangement, which could be changed at will to serve a variety of functions as needs arose over time (for working, entertaining, cooking and dining, and so on).

R. M. Schindler studio, ca. 1925–27. Note the use of the concrete pad as the studio floor and its extension into the court, linking interior and exterior space

Forming a concrete slab on the concrete pad, ca. March 15–30, 1922

Tilting a slab into place with the block and tackle, ca. March 28–April 24, 1922

31

The materials are products of the industrialized world employed uniformly on the exterior and interior in their unfinished state and natural color: concrete, glass, a machine-manufactured wallboard, machine-milled redwood, copper, and canvas. Yet Schindler's originality lay not so much in the newness of the materials as in the bold manner of their combination and the radical way they were used to create simple elemental forms. The building sits directly on a concrete slab that is both foundation and final floor, thus eliminating the need for expensive excavation and the construction of a basement. The tilt-up rectangular panels were fabricated on-site by pouring concrete into wood forms. Various membranes – soft soap, kraft paper, and burlap – were used to prevent adhesion to the slab; when cured, the panels were lifted into place using a tripod with a block and tackle. Visually they create a distinct vertical rhythm, as they are separated from each other by three-inch-wide strips of clear glass. The next step in the construction process was the erection around the concrete panels of a neutral cage of redwood, which was fitted with glass or Insulite panels.

Building the redwood framing and roof on the Marian Chace studio, ca. April 6–24, 1922

View out the guest studio toward Beverly Hills, ca. April 6, 1922

Casting the fireplace in Schindler's studio (at right), ca. May 1–10, 1922. From left to right, the garage, the guest studio, and the Schindler court and studios

The tilt-up panels (45 inches wide, 8½ feet high, tapering in thickness from 9½ inches at the bottom to 5 inches at the top) are bold in scale. The concrete is smooth and gray, the glass both clear and milky white (sandblasted), and the Insulite is tan. Each studio is screened from the garden by three translucent off-white canvas panels that can be slid across the opening or removed completely. These transparent, translucent, and opaque surfaces establish contrasts and interplays with one another as they are animated by natural light.

The idea of an opposition between concrete walls and non-load-bearing glass screens was the direct result of accommodating the building to its site, a suburban rectangular parcel bordered by neighbors on three sides and open to the street on the fourth. The structure is set back in the middle of the lot, but extends on the sides almost to the property line. In tune with the mild California climate, Schindler's main objective was to open the building to light, views, and the gardens while providing complete privacy for the occupants.

The building plan is a pinwheel of three L-shaped arms that pivot around a double fireplace, which is in the form of a rotated square.[33] While the dynamic rotation anticipates later works by Mies (as in his project for a concrete country house, 1923)[34] and Gropius (such as his Bauhaus Building, Dessau, 1925–26), the plan's only precedents are those of two structures – the director's residence and apartment building designed in 1920 for Wright's Olive Hill plan, possibly by Schindler, but never built.

The most important features of the plan are the visual axes, many of which are diagonal and constantly shift as the visitor moves through the spaces. At the entrance to the Schindler wing, a strong diagonal axis cuts through a glass corner from the hall to the court. In four of the studios (Clyde Chace, Marian Chace, R. M. Schindler, and the guest studio) projecting glass corners define but do not contain space and establish an unbroken connection between interior and exterior.

Underlying the entire composition is a three-dimensional geometric grid: a four-foot cubic module (the horizontal grid is clearly visible on the 1922 presentation

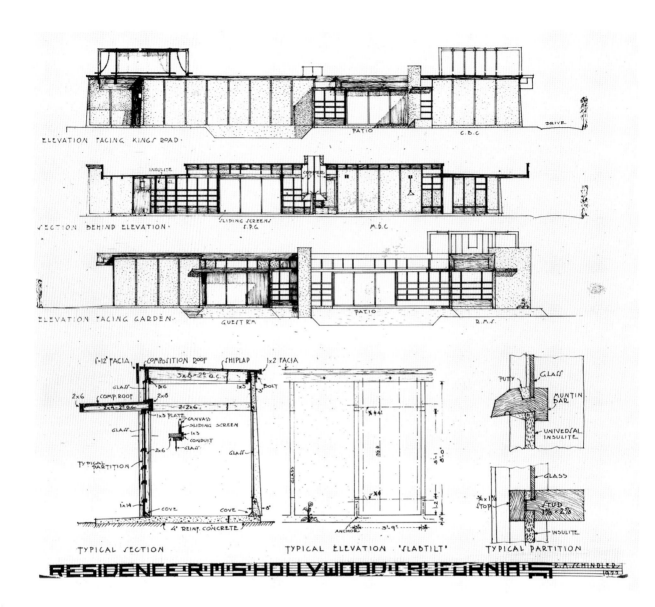

ELEVATION FACING KINGS ROAD.

PATIO

C.D.C.

DRIVE

SECTION BEHIND ELEVATION.

INSULITE

COPPER

SLIDING SCREENS
S.P.G

M.D.C.

ELEVATION FACING GARDEN.

GUEST R'M

PATIO

R.M.S.

TYPICAL SECTION

1×12 FACIA   COMPOSITION ROOF   SHIPLAP   1×2 FACIA

3×8 - 2° O.C.
GLASS   1×6   1×3   BOLT
2×6   COMP. ROOF   2×8
2-2×6.
2×4-2° O.C.
1×3 PLATE   CANVASS
GLASS   SLIDING SCREEN
1×3   CONDUIT
2×6   GLASS
TYPICAL   GLASS   GLASS
PARTITION
1×14   COVE   COVE   6"
4" REINF. CONCRETE

TYPICAL ELEVATION 'SLABTILT'

GLASS   ANCHOR.

TYPICAL PARTITION

PUTTY   GLASS
MUNTIN BAR
UNIVERSAL INSULITE

GLASS
STOP   STUD
INSULITE

RESIDENCE R·M·S·HOLLYWOOD·CALIFORNIA'S   R.M.SCHINDLER 1922

Elevations, section, and details, 1922

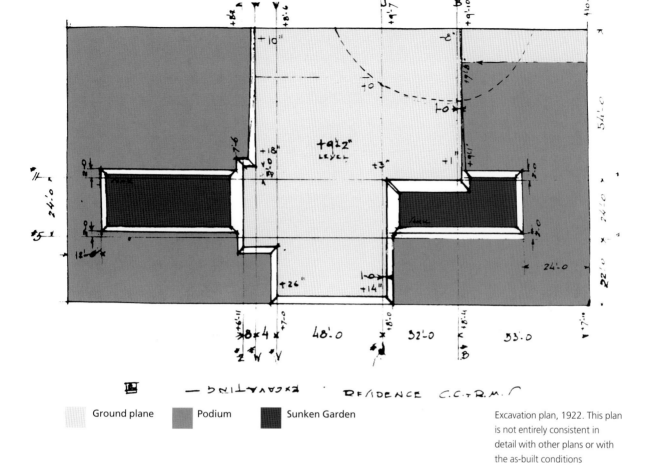

Ground plane   Podium   Sunken Garden

Excavation plan, 1922. This plan is not entirely consistent in detail with other plans or with the as-built conditions

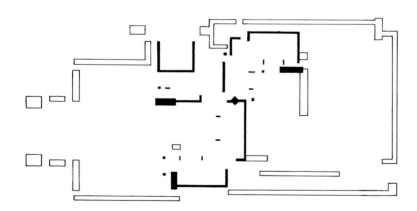

Diagram of the structure (dark lines) and landscape screens

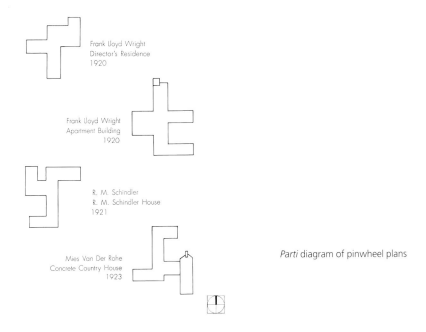

Frank Lloyd Wright
Director's Residence
1920

Frank Lloyd Wright
Apartment Building
1920

R. M. Schindler
R. M. Schindler House
1921

Mies Van Der Rohe
Concrete Country House
1923

Parti diagram of pinwheel plans

plan). Vertical space in the building is defined by the ceiling and a cantilevered over-hang. Every room, with the exception of the bathrooms, rises to a height of 8 feet 8 inches. A second level of 6 feet 3 inches is defined in the entry hall by the ceiling and in the studios by pairs of 2 x 6 tie beams that connect the concrete panels to the opposing redwood posts and carry the flat overhang beyond the glass walls. Where the edges of the ceiling and eave align vertically, Schindler placed a band of glass, creating a clerestory. In a radical departure from tradition (and even from Wright), Schindler eliminated references to doors, windows, and walls, transforming the one-story structure into a composition of transparent and solid vertical planes bounded by two horizontal planes – the flat roof and the concrete slab. He created a build-ing that was an expression of the new art of the century: geometric abstraction.

Perhaps the most radical idea behind the Kings Road house was Schindler's con-ception of the entire plot as the architectural field, which meant dispensing with a figure-ground relationship and thus giving equal weight to building and landscape. The living areas – the building, three courtyards, guest terrace, and driveway – sit several feet above the ground plane on a raised surface, as if on a podium. The height of this surface varies along the north-south axis due to the natural topography of the site, which slopes to the southwest. Further dynamism is created by a third plane, two feet lower than the ground plane, in the form of two rectangular sunken gar-dens situated on an east-west axis.

Schindler extended his spatial exploration into the surroundings by treating the gardens with a geometric precision equal to that applied in the building. The materials for both the structure and the landscape can be considered in hierarchical order, from mass to dematerialized screen: four large concrete blocks (the chimneys);

seven blocks, equally massive, of giant bamboo; bamboo hedges and concrete walls; wallboard in redwood framing; privet hedges; high grass; canvas panels; and large planes of glass. The gardens continue the same aesthetic themes expressed in the house, but with a greater sense of liberation. Vertical planes extend out into space, most as freestanding screens of green-gold bamboo or emerald-green privet hedge. The gardens were unprecedented: overlapping geometric planes creating a free plan – a work of modern art in nature.

By the end of the 1920s many of these features would be widely recognized as fundamental principles of modern architecture and ultimately used to define the International Style. This fact raises the question of why the Schindler House was not recognized for its originality and modernity while the architect was still alive.

The Schindler House in History

During the twentieth century the Schindler House was not generally acknowledged as one of the major achievements of modern architecture. At the time of its completion it was virtually unknown; it was not published until 1932, and due to its geographic distance from New York and Europe it had few influential visitors.

However, failure to perceive the building's value should not be attributed simply to its location. In his book *Modern Architecture: Romanticism and Reintegration* (1929), Henry-Russell Hitchcock, Jr., dismissed Schindler with one sentence by proclaiming, "He has paralleled with mediocre success the more extreme aesthetic researches of Le Corbusier and the men of de Stijl."[35] There were fifty-eight illustrations in Hitchcock's book, not one of them a Schindler building. Stung by a rebuke from a writer he did not know and who, presumably, had never seen his buildings in person, he wrote to Hitchcock in January 1930, "Your statement concerning my work is careless as you can not have any real knowledge of it. I have published hardly any of it, knowing that my architectural problem can not be reproduced on paper."[36] It would be possible to overlook the significance of this publication by assuming that Hitchcock was not familiar with work west of New York. This simply was not the case. Among the illustrations he included was a drawing by Neutra, whom he singled out in his text as the most important foreign architect working in America.[37]

Three years later, Hitchcock, this time working in collaboration with Philip Johnson under the institutional umbrella of The Museum of Modern Art in New York, would seal Schindler's fate for almost twenty years.[38] On an extended trip through Europe in the summer of 1930, Hitchcock and Johnson hit upon the idea of revising *Modern Architecture: Romanticism and Reintegration* for a general audience, using better illustrations. As they toured Germany, France, and Holland they added a component to the project: an exhibition on modern architecture. However, the show was assembled based solely on aesthetic criteria; Hitchcock and Johnson deliberately avoided technological and social issues. As plans progressed the two curators began to single out (ironically for Schindler) 1922 as the defining moment for modern architecture and to focus principally on the work of Mies, Le Corbusier, and Gropius.[39]

For all the intellectual rigor that Hitchcock and Johnson brought to their work, they were electrified by the energetic self-promotion of the avant-garde architects they had met in Europe. Carrying this enthusiasm back home, the authors sought to apply a critical viewpoint to a subject largely unknown in America. In *The International Style: Architecture since 1922,* the book that accompanied the exhibition, they outlined the main visual features of the new style: emphasis on volume rather than mass, regularity over symmetry, and the avoidance of applied ornament.[40]

The exhibition opened at The Museum of Modern Art in February 1932. When Schindler learned that the show would travel to Los Angeles, he wrote to Johnson, who replied to his inquiry on March 17, 1932, "From your letter and from my knowledge of your work, my real opinion is that your work would not belong in the Exhibition."[41] Since the Schindler House certainly fit all the major criteria set forth by the curators, one can only wonder why Johnson so emphatically rejected Schindler. In a 1988 interview Johnson explained, "I went to Los Angeles in 1931, primarily to see Richard Neutra, before the 'Modern Architecture' exhibition. Neutra was really evil, bad-mouthed everybody, especially Schindler. I went to see Schindler at his house. I didn't like the house, it looked cheap and the housekeeping wasn't good. Based on these impressions and what Neutra said, I didn't go to see anything else by Schindler."[42]

Ironically and tragically, the first systematic appraisal of Schindler's oeuvre took place a year after his death, when Esther McCoy and John Reed organized a memorial retrospective that opened in 1954 at the Landau Gallery in Los Angeles. Among the numerous tributes provided, Johnson's is noteworthy: "R. M. Schindler was among the great pioneers of modern architecture in this country. His work was not only great in itself, but had a lasting influence for good in later modern development. His single-minded devotion to the main principles of architecture was extraordinary and should serve as an example to the younger architects of our time."[43]

Almost twenty years after Johnson did so, Hitchcock had an opportunity to revise his earlier position. Writing in the preface to David Gebhard's monograph on Schindler, published in 1972, he stated, "I am glad that this [preface] gives me an opportunity to make some redress for the narrow-minded approach to Schindler, and indeed to modern architecture in California more generally, of a generation ago."[44] And more than two decades later, in 1995, Johnson went a step further when he wrote, "Rudolf [sic] M. Schindler was badly overlooked during his lifetime, and I must confess my part of it. I thought that Richard Neutra represented much more clearly the International Style which I was busy propagating at The Museum of Modern Art where I was the curator. Now I believe that Schindler was a much more important figure than I had casually assumed. His place at the crossroads of art and architecture and his variety and originality of design are much greater than I gave him credit for."[45]

There is even more poignant irony in the fact that the first and only time Schindler published the Kings Road house was the same month and year the International Style exhibition opened at MoMA – February 1932.[46] The minimal presentation – a ground plan, one exterior and one interior photograph, and an architect's brief (see Appendix B) – occupied a mere two pages in the professional journal *T-Square,* and it was virtually ignored. In one fell swoop national recognition of both his career and his first masterpiece was lost in the clamor over the newly discovered European International Style. While it is clear that Schindler's reputation has risen in the last three decades of the twentieth century, recognition of the Schindler House in particular has been slower to materialize.[47]

The Modern House

There is one particular feature of the Schindler House that clearly distinguishes it as the first modern house to be built in the world: its audacious originality given the years of its design and construction, 1921–22. However, this is the same fact that has been the main drawback to an understanding of its importance in the history of modern architecture. In other words, the house just did not *look* like anything else of its time.

As the history of the genesis of the International Style exhibition proves, by 1930 Hitchcock and Johnson had visited a number of buildings in Europe with common visual characteristics: strip windows, horizontal planes, flat roofs, metal railings, and grids of supports. Le Corbusier's Villa Savoye in Poissy, France (1928–29), Mies's Tugendhat House in Brno, Czechoslovakia (1930), and Gropius's Masters Houses for the Bauhaus in Dessau (1925–26) are just the most famous examples. Hitchcock

From left to right, Schindler studios and Chace studios, summer 1922

and Johnson were intent from the beginning on narrowing their argument to a definition of style, thereby rejecting anything that did not fit.

If issues of technology or social housing had formed part of the critical viewpoint, the Schindler House would have been harder to ignore. But even if we acknowledge that Hitchcock and Johnson were determined to codify modern architecture according to visual terms only, there is still no doubt that the Schindler House fell within the parameters of their definition. However, there was another unstated principle that unified the most seminal works in the MoMA show: the *idea* of the transformation of walls (exterior or interior) into non-load-bearing partitions by employing a frame (whether reinforced concrete or steel); and it was clear that to be modern it was necessary to make a distinct visual separation between the walls and the slender columns. By using large-scale concrete panels as the major structural support, the Schindler House did not conform to this criterion. From the distance of the twenty-first century, it is obvious that the current definition of modern architecture has greater flexibility and deeper meaning. It is within this broader perspective that the Schindler House can now be judged.

The Schindler House is different from the houses by Schindler's contemporaries and is unique even within his own oeuvre. As Banham pointed out in 1971, "The house [Schindler] built for himself and Clyde Chase [sic] in 1921 transcends, in my estimation, anything done by anybody (including himself) before Le Corbusier's Villa Savoye of 1930."[48] As a member of the first generation of modern architects, Schindler was motivated by revolutionary fervor; he longed to create a new house for the modern world. There is a very simple reason why he was the first to do it. Although the theoretical foundation existed in the work of others at the same moment, especially in the designs of Le Corbusier, between 1918 and 1922 construction in Europe and Russia was meager in the wake of economic, political, and social turmoil stemming from World War I and the Russian Revolution. Schindler had the ideas; he also had the means to realize them.

The Schindler House is a modern masterpiece – in its plan, its materials, its construction system, and, not least, in its spatial relationships. Modernism as an architectural movement is most closely associated with Europe, but it was given form and life first in the United States. As Banham has said, "There are plenty of learned pundits around who will point out that there can never be a genuinely fresh start in architecture, that it is improper to suppose that anyone could design a house as if there had never been houses before. Yet the Schindler House comes disturbingly near to being a totally new beginning."[49]

Notes

1 The process of defining modern architecture has been evolving since the early twentieth century. Whether we follow the pioneers, such as Nikolaus Pevsner, Henry-Russell Hitchcock, Jr., and Sigfried Giedion, or later writers, including Reyner Banham, Colin Rowe, and Kenneth Frampton, it is evident that there still is no consensus on the principles of modernism. On the contrary, there is disagreement and debate. For the purposes of this essay, I am using the following generally accepted criteria: Modern architecture should be based on new methods and materials, specifically those associated with industrial production; forms should be devoid of historical ornamentation and precedent; and plans and spaces should arise from the experiences of modern life.

2 Reyner Banham, "The Master Builders: 5," *The Sunday Times Magazine* (London) Aug. 8, 1971, 26.

3 It is essential to note that experimentation was taking place in Europe and the United States concurrently. Frank Lloyd Wright's place in the modern movement has often been a subject of spirited discussion. His house for Mrs. Thomas Gale constructed in 1909 was an abstract composition that was probably intended for cast concrete but was built of stucco and wood. Wright conceived plans for an all-concrete "Fireproof House" in 1907 and "American System-Built Houses" for mass production in dimensioned lumber in 1915–17, but neither of these schemes was executed as Wright originally intended. The first concrete textile-block houses were not built until 1923. (William Allin Storrer, *The Frank Lloyd Wright Companion*, Chicago: The University of Chicago Press, 1993.) Le Corbusier had formulated ideas for the Citrohan House in 1920 but did not build them until he started work on plans for a house for Georges Besnus at Vaucresson and a studio for Amédée Ozenfant in January 1923. (Tim Benton, *The Villas of Le Corbusier*, New Haven and London:

Yale University Press, 1987, 218.) Walter Gropius was addressing the problem at the Bauhaus, but his Sommerfeld House, designed in 1920 and built of wood planks in 1921, was stylistically derived from Wright's Winslow House of 1893. The more forward-looking "Experimental House am Horn" was designed in 1922 and built in 1923. (Winfried Nerdinger, *Walter Gropius*, Cambridge, Mass.: Busch-Reisinger Museum, 1985, 58–61.) Ludwig Mies van der Rohe's famous designs for a concrete country house and a brick country house have been dated 1922–23, but Mies was unable to realize his ideas until the end of the 1920s with the Barcelona Pavilion and the Tugendhat House. (Wolf Tegethoff, *Mies van der Rohe: The Villas and Country Houses*, New York: The Museum of Modern Art, 1985, 15–99.) Gerrit Rietveld in collaboration with Truus Schröder began the design of the de Stijl masterwork, the Schröder House, in early 1924; it was completed at the end of the year. (Paul Overy, *The Rietveld Schröder House*, Amsterdam: Thoth, 1992, 17.)

4 Banham, "The Master Builders: 5," 26.

5 William Reichert, letter to R. M. Schindler, Dec. 11, 1913, Architectural Drawing Collection, University Art Museum, University of California, Santa Barbara (hereinafter referred to as UCSB).

6 R. M. Schindler, letter to Richard Neutra, no date, ca. Mar. 1914, in Esther McCoy, *Vienna to Los Angeles: Two Journeys. Letters between R. M. Schindler and Richard Neutra* (Santa Monica, Calif.: Arts + Architecture Press, 1979), 104.

7 R. M. Schindler, letter to Frank Lloyd Wright, no date, ca. Nov. 23, 1914, Frank Lloyd Wright correspondence with R. M. Schindler, 1914–29, The Getty Research Institute for the History of Art and the Humanities, Special Collections and Visual Resources, Accession No. 960076 (hereinafter referred to as Getty Institute), Box 1, Folder 3, Document 31040.

8 Frank Lloyd Wright, "In the Cause of Architecture," *Architectural Record* 23 (Mar. 1908), 157.

9 Harry Robinson for Frank Lloyd Wright, letter to Mrs. Avery Coonley, Dec. 30, 1914, Getty Institute, Box 1, Folder 3, Document 31039.

10 R. M. Schindler, letter to Richard Neutra, no date, ca. Dec. 1920–Jan. 1921, in McCoy, 129.

11 Richard Neutra, letter to R. M. Schindler, Sept. 20, 1919, in McCoy, 113.

12 In a letter to staff at his downtown Chicago office building Wright gave permission for Schindler to use his office in the last months of 1917. (Frank Lloyd Wright, letter to Misses Kimbell, Hazelton, and Wigginton, Oct. 20, 1917, Getty Institute, Box 1, Folder 3, Document 31042.) Supervision of the Buena Shore Club ended December 31, 1917. Schindler's surviving notes on his employment with Wright, however, indicate that he did not start work on salary for Wright until February 1918. (UCSB.) Wright indicated that he was going on a trip beginning November 1917; the destination of his trip is unknown, but all evidence points to the fact that he did not go to Japan during those months. ("Minister's House Demolished," *Japan Advertiser*, Nov. 18, 1917, 3.)

13 R. M. Schindler, letter to Richard Neutra, no date, ca. Dec. 1920–Jan. 1921, in McCoy, 130.

14 Frank Lloyd Wright, letter to R. M. Schindler, no date, ca. 1919, Getty Institute, Box 1, Folder 5, Document 31037.

15 Wright's prolonged absences in Japan in the 1910s and early 1920s are comparable, with one crucial difference, to the period 1909–10, when he spent most of his time in Europe. While he was in Japan he did not close his office, and Schindler was left in charge of his affairs in America. In 1931 an open dispute surfaced between Wright and Schindler over Schindler's role in Wright's office while he was in Japan. Wright had received a circular from the Chouinard Art Institute, sent at Schindler's request, announcing a class to be taught by Schindler and Neutra. In the circular, Schindler's biography stated that he had been in charge of Wright's office during Wright's absence

in Japan. On June 3, 1931, Wright wrote to Schindler objecting to this statement. On June 10, 1931, Schindler responded to Wright, claiming, among other things, that he executed seven commissions, including those for the Hardy Monolith Home, during those years. He wrote, "All these projects were started after your departure and drawn without your presence and help." In a letter to his son Lloyd Wright on June 19, 1931, Wright does admit, "The only sketches R. S. made I know anything about are the Hardy cottages he refers to." In his response to Schindler on the same day he stated, "Where I am my office is. My office is me. Frank Lloyd Wright has no other office, never had one and never will have one. You know it damned well." In 1941 Henry-Russell Hitchcock, Jr., worked closely with Wright on the preparation of a monograph of his work titled *In the Nature of Materials*. In the "Chronological List of Buildings and Projects" the following statement appears next to the listing for the Monolith Homes: "This scheme, as well as the C. E. Staley and J. P. Shampay house projects of this year were developed by R. M. Schindler during Wright's absence in Japan. They are hardly to be considered Wright's work, though they issued from his office and the Monolith drawings carry his signature." (Henry-Russell Hitchcock, Jr., *In the Nature of Materials*, New York: Duell, Sloan and Pearce, 1942, 123.) In November 1941 Wright came to Kings Road to apologize, but Schindler was not in. Pauline Schindler, however, took the message. The last contact between the two was in 1953, when Wright, at Pauline's suggestion, wrote Schindler a note of sympathy a month before Schindler died. (Frank Lloyd Wright Archives, Taliesin West, Scottsdale, Ariz., and UCSB.)

16 Sophie Pauline Gibling Schindler, letter to Mr. and Mrs. Edmund J. Gibling, no date, ca. July 24, 1920, photocopy in possession of the author.

17 R. M. Schindler, School of Architecture, University of Southern California, Los Angeles, Oct. 10, 1949, in August Sarnitz, *R. M. Schindler, Architect: 1887–1953* (New York: Rizzoli, 1988), 68.

18 On April 30, 1921, Pauline Schindler wrote her parents that Irving Gill had come to dinner, thus indicating they had an acquaintance before the Chaces arrived. Lloyd Wright could have been a likely connection as he had worked for Gill between 1912 and 1914. Gill first began using the tilt-slab method in 1912. It had been invented by Robert Aiken, who patented the system in 1908. (Thomas S. Hines, *Irving Gill and the Architecture of Reform: A Study in Modernist Architectural Culture*, New York: Monacelli, 2000, 124.) On November 27, 1921, Lloyd Wright and Gill reviewed the plans for the Schindler House. (Sophie Pauline Gibling Schindler, letter to Mr. and Mrs. Edmund J. Gibling, Nov. 27, 1921, UCSB.)

19 On December 28, 1921, the lot was purchased for $2750 from Walter Luther Dodge (owner of the Gill house on the same street), with the Schindlers putting up $2350 and the Chaces $400. The two couples signed an agreement to build together on February 11, 1922. Although the Schindlers owned a greater share by virtue of their larger financial investment, the Chaces agreed to buy their one-half interest within two years.

20 R. M. Schindler, letter to Mr. and Mrs. Edmund J. Gibling, Nov. 26, 1921, Friends of the Schindler House, courtesy of the Schindler Family. In 1949 Schindler further explained his goals: "You understand that Kings Road was built as a protest against the American habit of covering their life and their buildings with coats of finish material to fool the onlooker about the commonplace base." (R. M. Schindler, letter to Pauline Schindler, Apr. 8, 1949, UCSB.)

21 Ibid.

22 R. M. Schindler, letter to Sophie Pauline Gibling Schindler, Apr. 20, 1922, photocopy in possession of the author.

23 Residence CC/RMS, Estimate of Cost, Dec. 1921, UCSB.

24 There are three surviving drawings for furniture: a sling chair, a canvas chair, and the one-leg table. Robert Sweeney concludes that the seventeen surviving pieces of furniture for the Schindler House were designed by Schindler. Author, interview with Robert Sweeney, Mar. 1, 2000.

25 R. M. Schindler, letter to Mr. and Mrs. Edmund J. Gibling, Apr. 24, 1922, photocopy in possession of the author.

26 A Notice of Completion was filed on June 6, 1922.

27 Schindler's term "slab-tilt" (a variation of the established phrase "tilt-slab") referred to the process of pouring concrete into modular molds on the site and tilting them in place when dry. "Slab-cast" was a term he used to describe what is more generally known as slip-form construction. Wood planks are built on two sides with a cavity in the middle to create a vertical wall, concrete is poured between the wood planks, dried, and the molds are moved up the wall in sections, more concrete is poured, and so forth, until a monolithic wall is constructed. The grain of the wood boards often leaves a pattern on the surface, as well as thin ridges where the boards met at their edges.

28 Archival photographs indicate that the Chace sleeping basket was built before their departure; however, an exact date has not been determined for its construction. I am grateful to Robert Sweeney for this information.

29 The Schindler-Chace agreement was dissolved on July 26, 1924.

30 Schindler met Neutra on May 29, 1924, en route to New York to work for a client, Helena Rubenstein, who lived in Connecticut. Neutra was in Chicago awaiting the arrival of his wife and son.

31 In a letter to Mr. and Mrs. Edmund Gibling dated November 26, 1921, Schindler used the term "utility room." However, on the presentation plan drawn in 1922, he used the word "kitchen" to designate the same room.

32 Sophie Pauline Gibling Schindler was known by various names during

different periods of her life. In the early years of her marriage, she did not change her name; the presentation drawing as a result calls out her studio as that of SPG. Marian Chace called her by a nickname, Gibbi, and the Neutras called her Ghibbeline. Later in her life, she was known as Pauline Schindler. For consistency, I use the latter name throughout this text.

33 Although Schindler's plan is clearly asymmetrical and does not follow classical principles using a primary and secondary axis for the building plan, the plot plan (laid out on a four-foot grid) does have a primary and secondary axis, which cross at the central passage between the Pauline Schindler studio, the Marian Chace studio, and the utility room. The plan, as a result, pivots around both a solid (the double fireplace) and a void (the passage). I am indebted to Grant Mudford for making this apparent to me.

34 Lionel March speculates that Mies could have seen Schindler's drawings for the Kings Road house while in Berlin in 1922. March further posits that Schindler may have sent a set of his drawings to Neutra, who was working at that time for Erich Mendelsohn, who often discussed progressive architectural innovations with Mies. (Yukio Futagawa, ed. and photog., and Lionel March, *Rudolph M. Schindler, R. M. Schindler House, Hollywood, California, 1921–22; James E. How House, Los Angeles, California, 1925, GA 77*, Tokyo: A.D.A. Edita, 1999, unpag.)

35 Henry-Russell Hitchcock, Jr., *Modern Architecture: Romanticism and Reintegration* (New York: Payson and Clarke, 1929), 204–5.

36 R. M. Schindler, letter to Henry-Russell Hitchcock, Jr., Jan. 1930, UCSB.

37 Hitchcock, *Modern Architecture*, 204 and pl. 58.

38 This result ironically recalls Schindler's letter to the Giblings, Apr. 24, 1922, in which he predicted the house would either attract or repulse people.

39 Terence Riley, *The International Style: Exhibition 15 and The Museum of Modern Art* (New York: Rizzoli, 1992), 12–27.

40 Henry-Russell Hitchcock, Jr., and Philip Johnson, with a preface by Alfred H. Barr, Jr., *The International Style: Architecture since 1922* (New York, W. W. Norton, 1932), 13.

41 Philip Johnson, letter to R. M. Schindler, Mar. 17, 1932, in Sarnitz, 209.

42 Johnson quoted in Sweeney, 38.

43 Johnson quoted in Sarnitz, 215.

44 Henry-Russell Hitchcock, Jr., preface, in David Gebhard, *Schindler* (New York: Viking, 1972), 8.

45 Philip Johnson, untitled, in *MAK Center for Art and Architecture, R. M. Schindler*, ed. Peter Noever (Munich and New York: Prestel, 1995), 27.

46 *Architectural Record* rejected publication of the Schindler House in 1930. In response to the editor, Schindler pointed out, "[The building] does not look 'modern' in the cut and dried fashion of all your recent importations." He continued, "It initiates a development in residence building which was recently furthered by Mies van der Rohe in his Model Residence at the German Building Exposition. Although my house is speaking in different materials a different language, it says essentially the same thing." (R. M. Schindler, letter to Maxwell Levinson, Jan. 20, 1931, UCSB.) I am indebted to Judith Sheine for these references.

47 Schindler scholarship began with the work of Esther McCoy, whose several essays published in the 1950s culminated in her landmark book, *Five California Architects* (1960). At her suggestion, Schindler's papers were deposited by his family at UCSB, which made future scholarship possible. McCoy's perceptive analysis of Schindler's work spurred interest in Europe and the United States. Most noteworthy were an essay by Hans Hollein in *Der Aufbau* (1961) and the work of David Gebhard: an exhibition and catalogue (1967) followed by a major monograph (1972). By the late 1960s and early 1970s a consensus began to build that Schindler's masterpiece was the Lovell House. The notable exception to this trend was Reyner Banham, who was the first to focus on the Schindler House as the architect's best work while declaring that "modern architecture would have happened in California even if de Stijl, Corbu, Mies, Gropius and The Museum of Modern Art had never existed." (Reyner Banham, "Pioneering without Tears," *Architectural Design* 37, Dec. 1967, 578.) The more recent in-depth studies by August Sarnitz, Lionel March, and Judith Sheine have begun to propel Schindler to the forefront of first-generation modern architects. Aside from scholarly assessments, the most obvious reason for the rising interest in the Schindler House is due to the fact that a nonprofit organization, Friends of the Schindler House, purchased the property from the family in 1980, and under the direction of Robert Sweeney carried out extensive restoration of the house and gardens and initiated public tours. Beginning with the centennial of Schindler's birth, in 1987, several articles by Sweeney and this author appeared explaining the history and significance of the house. Under Sweeney's direction the property has regained its architectural integrity and now reflects Schindler's original intentions for the first time since the 1940s.

48 Banham, "The Master Builders: 5," 26.

49 Ibid.

Photograph Portfolio Grant Mudford

Unless otherwise noted, the
following photographs show
the house with the sliding
canvas panels removed, and
all the furniture was designed
by R. M. Schindler.

View from Schindler studios hall
into R. M. Schindler studio. In the
middle ground, the Cube chair

Pauline Schindler studio, with
Schindler sleeping basket above

Entrance to Schindler studios,
with diagonal view through the
hall into the court

View from R. M. Schindler studio
into Pauline Schindler studio. On
the right, the door to the Schindler
sleeping basket has been closed

Schindler studios hall, with Pauline
Schindler studio to the left, and
stair to the Schindler sleeping basket
to the right. On the central post, a
recessed light fixture behind opaque
glass, with pull chain

View from R. M. Schindler
studio across the court to the
guest studio and utility room

R. M. Schindler studio. From
left to right, one-leg table, Cube
chairs, and ottomans

Pauline Schindler studio on the
left, R. M. Schindler's on the right,
sleeping basket above

View from Pauline Schindler studio toward R. M. Schindler studio. In the foreground, Schindler's bench; in the background, his Cube chair and model of the Wolfe House (1928)

Pauline Schindler studio with door
open to the central passage; the
utility room is in the background,
center. From left to right, bench,
sofa, and one-leg table with stool

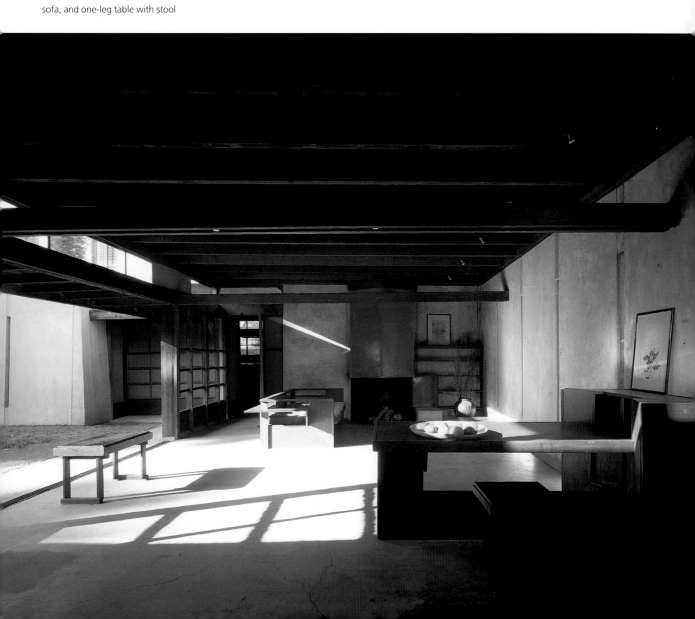

Pauline Schindler studio, with
ottomans and Cube chair, and
view of court

From left to right, Pauline Schindler studio, sleeping basket, and R. M. Schindler studio. Through the glass corner, one sees out the front door, which is ajar

Schindler sleeping basket

View of R. M. Schindler studio
from the roof

Schindler bathroom. Counter and
tub lining are made of magnesite

Chace studios viewed from the sunken garden

From left to right, Marian Chace studio, Chace nursery, and Clyde Chace studio; sleeping basket is above

View, from the roof, over Marian
Chace studio (with glass corner)
to Schindler studios

Clyde Chace studio. The silk curtain screens a closet

Chace sleeping basket. Clyde Chace studio is visible below, through the clerestory window

Clyde Chace studio, looking
toward Marian Chace studio

Clyde Chace studio with view of
sunken garden and freestanding
hedge screens beyond

View from Clyde Chace studio,
across the court and past the
nursery, to Marian Chace studio.
From left to right, bench, children's
chairs, and Cube chair

Marian Chace studio, with view
into the bathroom at right.
The folding chairs are from the
Gordon House (1950)

Marian Chace studio, with view
through the glass corner to the
sunken garden

Pages 66–67: View from Marian
Chace studio to the nursery and
Clyde Chace studio

Marian Chace studio. In the
background, to the left, is the
central passage with the door
open to the Schindler court

View from the central passage
between Pauline Schindler
studio and the utility room; the
back door to the guest studio
is straight ahead

R. M. Schindler studio, with
children's chair, bench, and
Cube chair

Pauline Schindler studio, viewed
from the court

Pauline Schindler studio

Pages 74–75: Pauline Schindler
studio, furnished with sofa,
ottomans, Cube chair, and one-leg
table. Parchment pyramid lamps
hang from tie beams. The swinging
door to the utility room is closed.
Across the court are an outdoor fireplace and the guest studio

Fireplace with copper hood in
Pauline Schindler studio

R. M. Schindler studio. In the glass
bay are a model of the Wolfe
House (1928) and a parchment
pyramid lamp

Pages 78–79: Chace studios
and sleeping basket

View of Chace studios with
the canvas panels in place and the
door to the nursery closed

Appendix A
R. M. Schindler, Los Angeles, letter to Mr. and Mrs. Edmund J. Gibling, Evanston, Illinois, November 26, 1921

Los Angeles, Cal.
Nov. 26th 1921 —
[no salutation]

From S. P. G. I hear that it may be possible to actively interest you in our venture – and therefore am sending you prints of our first sketches – which will give a better idea of the scheme than a letter. The basic idea was to give each person his own room – instead of the usual distribution – and to do most of the cooking right on the table – making it more of a social "campfire" affair, than the disagreeable burden to one member of the family – for special occasions, as well as for all household work which needs expensive equipment (laundry, etc.) the "utility room" is provided, containing a complete kitchen and laundry equipment storage bins, icebox etc. which shall be used by inhabitants in common. The utility room therefore must be in the center of the structure.

The rooms are large studiorooms – with concrete walls on three sides, the front open (glass) to the outdoors – a real California scheme. On the roof two "sleeping baskets" are provided – for openair sleeping – with a temporary cover for rainy nights. The "guest room" is to be rented out – has its own bath and kitchen and garden, and will insure the paying of taxes, interest, etc. at all times.

Both "court" and "terrace" are to be used for social events – especially the court may be covered by a velumn [sic] and serve as a real room. Both have fireplaces.

The concrete floors and concrete walls will form an everlasting backbone for the structure – the concrete being properly finished, all plaster has been done away with, which insures a low upkeep for the whole. The gravel roof used too is the most durable of all modern protectors against the rain. To meet all objections of the "practical" real estate man, I have shown with how little extra expense the building may be turned into a "conventional residence" – insuring its salability at all times.

S. P. G.'s long letter seems to cover the rest of the ground – I shall be able to give definite figures in a few days – and hope that you will be convinced of the soundness of the enterprise. Of course the plan is to finish the building just enough to make it habitable and to do the rest, while we are living there ourselves – which is one of the main points, why it would be complicated to procure a mortgage from somebody who does not know us at all. Two firms however have already uttered their willingness to give us the mortgage – for ten years even – which shows that they do not think the present interest rate of 8% will last much longer – and that the investment is a good one.

We shall get definite cost estimates presently – and keep you informed of our progress – hoping that we actually will progress rapidly – RMS

Appendix B
R. M. Schindler, "A Cooperative Dwelling," *T-Square* 2 (February 1932), 20–21

Location: Lot facing east with slight slope towards the southwest.

Program: A cooperative dwelling for two young couples.

Layout: The ordinary residential arrangement providing rooms for specialized purposes has been abandoned. Instead each person receives a large private studio, each couple a common entrance hall and bath. Open porches on the roof are used for sleeping. An enclosed patio for each couple, with an out-of-door fireplace, serves the purposes of an ordinary living room. The form of the house divides the garden into several such private rooms. A separate guest apartment, with its own garden, is also provided for. One kitchen is planned for both couples. The wives take alternate weekly responsibility for dinner menus, and so gain periods of respite from the incessant household rhythm.

Structural Scheme: The house is constructed by the architect's "slab-tilt" system.

A reinforced concrete floor is placed on the ground. Low wooden frames and reinforcing rods are placed on it. The concrete wall units are poured between them in a horizontal position and finished on the top surface. After the concrete has set they are tilted up by means of a tripod with a block and tackle and easily handled by two men. Adhesion between wall and floor is prevented by a coating of soft soap on the floor before pouring the wall slabs. The wall slabs are graduated in thickness towards the top in order to save material. The form work required a three-inch space between wall units. This is either filled up with concrete or left partly open for glazing. The system provides a reinforced concrete wall, finished on both sides with a minimum of form work. A layer of insulating material could easily be introduced for colder climates.

The resulting wall has all the repose of the old type masonry wall without its heavy, confining qualities. It permits air and light to filter through the joints, wherever they are kept open. In this particular instance the ceilings are all made of exposed redwood timbers and shiplap covered with composition roofing. They are supported on one side of each room by the concrete walls, and on the other side by two wooden posts. All partitions and patio walls are non-supporting screens composed of a wooden skeleton filled in with glass or with removable "Insulite" panels. Clerestory windows between two ceiling levels, maintained throughout the house, provide a cooling air current right under the roof and permit the sunlight to enter from all sides. All doors are double-acting with pivots fastened to floor and lower ceiling.

Architectural scheme: Each room in the house represents a variation on one structural and architectural theme. This theme fulfills the basic requirements for a camper's shelter: a protected back, and open front, a fireplace, and roof.

Each room has a concrete wall for back, and a garden front with a large opening fitted with sliding doors. This opening is protected by an overhanging eave, carried by two cantilever beams crossing the rooms. These beams serve at the same time as supports for sliding light fixtures, and for additional moveable partitions.

The shape of the rooms, their relation to the patios and the alternating roof levels, create an entirely new spatial interlocking between the interior and the garden.

Materials: The traditional building scheme, by which the structural members of the house are covered onion-like with layers of finishing materials – lathe, plaster, paint, paper, hangings, etc. – is abandoned. The house is a simple weave of a few structural materials which retain their natural color and texture throughout. It is the beginning of a building system which a highly developed technical science will permit in the future. Each material will take its place openly in the structure, fulfilling all architectural and structural functions of its place in the organic fabric of the building.

Textures and Colors: Concrete: gray, smooth. Insulite: tan, rough like a textile. Wood: California redwood, natural redbrown, wirebrushed to accentuate the grain. Glass.

From left to right, Schindler studios, Chace studios. In the foreground, the sunken garden

Selected Bibliography

Banham, Reyner. "The Master Builders: 5." *The Sunday Times Magazine* (London), Aug. 8, 1971, 18–27.

——."Rudolph Schindler – A Pioneer without Tears." *Architectural Design* 37 (Dec. 1967), 578–79.

Futagawa, Yukio, ed. and photog., and Lionel March. *Rudolph M. Schindler, R. M. Schindler House, Hollywood, California, 1921–22; James E. How House, Los Angeles, California, 1925, GA* 77. Tokyo: A.D.A. Edita, 1999.

Gebhard, David. *Schindler.* Preface by Henry-Russell Hitchcock. New York: Viking, 1972.

Hines, Thomas S. "Conserving the Visible Past: The Schindler House and the Los Angeles Preservation Movement." *L.A. Architect* (Sept. 1978), unpag.

——. "Echoes of Olympus: The Historic Schindler House in West Hollywood." Photographs by Grant Mudford. *Angeles* (Aug. 1989), 87–95, 118.

——. *Richard Neutra and the Search for Modern Architecture: A Biography and History.* New York and Oxford, England: Oxford University Press, 1982.

Hollein, Hans. "R. M. Schindler – Ein Wiener Architekt in Kalifornien." *Der Aufbau* (Mar. 1961), 102–4.

McCoy, Esther. *Five California Architects.* New York: Reinhold, 1960.

——. "Schindler: A Personal Reminiscence." *L.A. Architect* (Nov. 1987), 5–9.

——. *Vienna to Los Angeles: Two Journeys. Letters between R. M. Schindler and Richard Neutra.* Foreword by Harwell Hamilton Harris. Santa Monica, Calif.: Arts + Architecture Press, 1979.

Neutra, Richard and Dione. *Richard Neutra, Promise and Fulfillment: 1919–1932. Selections from the Letters and Diaries of Richard and Dione Neutra.* Compiled and trans. by Dione Neutra. Carbondale and Edwardsville, Ill.: Southern Illinois University Press, 1986.

Noever, Peter, and Gerald Zugmann. *Zugmann: Schindler.* Photographs by Gerald Zugmann. Santa Monica, Calif.: Form Zero, 1996.

Sarnitz, August. *R. M. Schindler, Architect: 1887–1953.* New York: Rizzoli, 1988.

Schindler, R. M. "A Cooperative Dwelling." *T-Square* 2 (Feb. 1932), 20–21.

Sheine, Judith. *2G: R. M. Schindler, 10 Houses* 7. Additional texts by Margaret Crawford, Enric Miralles, and Michael Rotondi. Photographs by Grant Mudford. Barcelona: Gustavo Gili, 1998.

——. *Works and Projects: R. M. Schindler.* Photographs by Grant Mudford. Barcelona: Gustavo Gili, 1998.

Smith, Kathryn. "Chicago–Los Angeles: The Concrete Connection." *On Architecture, the City, and Technology,* ed. Marc M. Angelil. Stoneham, Mass.: Butterworth-Heineman, 1990, 103–5.

——. *Frank Lloyd Wright, Hollyhock House, Olive Hill: Buildings and Projects for Aline Barnsdall.* Photographs by Sam Nugroho. New York: Rizzoli, 1992.

——. "Frank Lloyd Wright and the Imperial Hotel: A Postscript." *The Art Bulletin* 67 (June 1985), 296–310.

——. "R. M. Schindler's House on Kings Road." *A* 1 (Summer 1976), 8–13.

——. "The Schindler House," photographs by Grant Mudford. In *R. M. Schindler: Composition and Construction,* ed. Lionel March and Judith Sheine. London: Academy Editions, 1993, 114–23.

——. *The Schindler House, 1921–22.* West Hollywood, Calif.: Friends of the Schindler House, 1987.

Sweeney, Robert L. "His House, Her House, Their House." In *MAK Center for Art and Architecture, R. M. Schindler,* ed. Peter Noever. Munich and New York: Prestel, 1995, 37–49.

——."A Real California Scheme." *GA Houses* 26. Tokyo: A.D.A. Edita, 1989, 6–27.

——. "Sophie Pauline Gibling Schindler Correspondence, The Architectural Drawing Collection, University of California, Santa Barbara, On Deposit by the Schindler Family, Inventory Prepared by Robert L. Sweeney, 1996–1999." 1999, photocopied typescript.

Acknowledgments

My awareness of the Schindler House dates to 1975, when I first interviewed Pauline Schindler while I was conducting research on Frank Lloyd Wright's commission for Aline Barnsdall. The pioneering publications of, first of all, Esther McCoy, and then a little later, David Gebhard, had prepared me for my encounter with the architecture, but not with Pauline Schindler herself. She filled the room with her presence, talking quietly but listening intensely. She spoke of R. M. Schindler but also of Wright and of Taliesin, where, she recalled, she had found the essentials of life: work, play, love, and worship. As I rose to leave, she inquired if I would like to live at the Schindler House. I answered without hesitation.

As a tenant (I lived in the sleeping basket above the Schindler studios; Mrs. Schindler occupied the Chace studios), I was gradually introduced to her family: her son, Mark, and his three children, Ian, Margot, and Eric. Sometime later I met Mark's former wife, Mary. Over the years each member of the family has generously shared with me both their memories and mementos of the Schindler House, for which I am grateful. It was also a joy to meet, some years later, Clyde Chace, and his daughter, Ann Harriett Eastwood, who returned to the house with their family photo album and graciously answered eager questions. Over the years numerous former tenants have supplied important information, and art historian Peg Weiss provided photos of Galka Scheyer from the Valeska Archives, which added a valuable dimension to the cultural history of the house.

Mrs. Schindler's unexpected death in 1977 led to the formation of a nonprofit organization, Friends of the Schindler House, which acquired the property from the family in 1980 in order to restore and preserve it. The struggles of the first phase of planning were overcome primarily through the efforts of Harriett Gold along with Peter Benzian of the law firm Latham and Watkins. Both remain today two of the most loyal supporters of FOSH. Throughout the years major contributions of effort and time have been made by Bernard Judge, David Gebhard, Michael Bobrow, Stefanos Polyzoides, John Mason Caldwell, Jim Johnson, Nancy J. Sanquist, Barbara Goldstein, Emmet Wemple, Charles W. Moore, and Ron Filson.

One day in 1976, I was in the R. M. Schindler studio when the telephone rang; it was Esther McCoy. She congratulated me on a short article I had written about the Schindler House that was called to her attention by Cesar Pelli. Over the next decade I learned more about the Schindler House from Esther than from anyone else; but what I learned was not confined to facts and dates. It is Esther who informs this book and to whom I owe the most.

In the twenty years since FOSH acquired the Schindler House, the dedication and guidance of its director, Robert L. Sweeney, have been of consummate importance. With the exception of Schindler and McCoy, there is probably no one else who is more single-handedly responsible for bringing this masterwork to international attention than Bob. Through his efforts the City of West Hollywood, the National Endowment for the Arts, and the Austrian Consulate have become loyal supporters. Bob's work on the restoration was the impetus behind the Schindler Centennial, which I organized in 1987. Special thanks must go to Robert Nicolais, who donated many hours toward restoration of the house and built all of the reproduction furniture. The centennial celebration was made possible by the generosity of Hans Hollein, Wolfgang Puck, Pelli, Randall Kennon, Buzz Yudell, Tina Beebe, Dana Levy, Letitia Burns O'Connor, Bette Wagner, and Ulf Pacher. The house was glowing on Schindler's birthday and has been in the days since because of the eternal vigilance of Isrrael Fuentes, Jr., and his successor, Omar Velazquez.

Coincidentally, during the planning of the centennial I was living at Richard Neutra's Kelton Apartments, where I met his sister-in-law, Regula Niedermann Fybel, and her husband, Hans. The Neutra family owned the building and Regula was the building manager. Through Regula, I came to know her sister, Dione Niedermann Neutra, and Dione's two sons, Dion and Raymond. Over the years the Neutra family have shared their archive of letters, photographs, and memories of Kings Road. They have enriched my knowledge and understanding of the Schindler-Neutra household during the 1920s. The highlight of my talks with Regula was the day I inquired if she had any photographs of the Kings Road house in her papers. With a hint of disappointment she responded, "No, but I do have a roll of motion pictures that Richard took when he lived there. Would they be of interest?" I rushed them off to a film restorer, and they came to occupy a prized place in the centennial exhibit.

An international connection was realized in 1994, when the MAK – Austrian Museum of Applied Arts, Vienna – entered into a ten-year cooperative agreement with FOSH. It is Peter Noever whose vision for the MAK Center for Art and Architecture, Los Angeles, has carried the house into the twenty-first century. Special recognition must be extended to the Federal Chancellery, Department of the Arts, and to the Federal Ministry of Education, Science, and Culture of the Republic of Austria for their continued support of this collaboration.

Grant Mudford more than anyone else has captured Schindler's vision on paper. Although Schindler often complained that it was impossible to convey his work in photographs, I think he would disagree if he saw the images by Grant featured in this book. The idea for this publication was Grant's, and I am grateful to him, and to Judith Sheine, who suggested we work together. Judith's enthusiasm for Schindler and her extensive knowledge of his career have broadened my education greatly. I would also like to extend thanks to Kurt Helfrich, Architectural Drawing Collection, University of California, Santa Barbara; Wim de Wit and his staff at Special Collections, the Getty Research Institute (especially Mark Henderson and Karin Lanzoni); Oscar Muñoz, Frank Lloyd Wright Archives, Taliesin West; John Franklin, UCLA Department of Geography; Katherine Floto Loverud; and Eulogio Guzman.

Grant and I extend our deepest appreciation to those who have helped us realize this book. The cooperation of Bob Sweeney, Peter Noever, Daniela Zyman, and LouAnne Greenwald at the MAK Center was invaluable. At Harry N. Abrams, Inc., Diana Murphy provided her editorial talents and generous sense of humor, and Judith Hudson has given the book a gracious feel to the eye and to the hand.

Kathryn Smith
Santa Monica, California

Index

Page numbers in italics refer to illustrations.

A

Adler and Sullivan, 9
Aiken, Robert, 42 n. 18
American System-Built Houses (Wright), 40 n. 3
Amerika (Neutra), 28
Architectural Group for Industry and Commerce, 27
Architectural Record, 43 n. 46
Austrian Museum of Applied Arts (Vienna), 85

B

Banham, Reyner, 7, 40, 40 n. 1, 43 n. 47
Barcelona Pavilion (Mies van der Rohe), 40 n. 3
Barnsdall, Aline, 14
Bauhaus, 40 n. 3
Bauhaus buildings (Gropius), 33, 39
Benzian, Peter, 84
Besnus House (Le Corbusier), 40 n. 3
Bethlehem Baptist Church (Schindler), 29
Blue Four, 28
Bovingdon, John, 28–29
Buena Shore Club clubhouse (Schindler), 10–11, 41 n. 12

C

Cage, John, 29
Chace, Clyde, 7, 18, 19, 26; Popenoe House, 25; Pueblo Ribera Courts, 25. *See also* Schindler House
Chace, Marian ("Kimmie"; *née* Marian Da Camara), 7, 18, 24, 25, 26. *See also* Schindler House
Chace nursery (Schindler House), 24, *58, 63, 66–67*
Chace studios (Schindler House), *6,* 7, 24, 26, *26–27,* 28, 29, *29, 39,* 42 n. 28, *58–67, 69, 77–79, 82*
Children's Workshop, 27
Chouinard Art Institute, 41 n. 15
Citrohan House (Le Corbusier), 40 n. 3
concrete: slab-cast (slip-form) method, 25, 42 n. 27; slab-tilt method, 25, 32, 42 n. 27; textile-block houses, 40 n. 3; tilt-slab method, 18, 42 n. 18
construction (Schindler House), 18, *22,* 24–25, 30, *31–36,* 32, 40, 42 nn. 27–28, 81
cooperative dwelling, 25–26, 27, 81

D

Da Camara, Marian. *See* Chace, Marian
design (Schindler House), 18–21, *20–21,* 24, 42 n. 24, 80–81
Dodge, Walter Luther, 42 n. 19
Dodge House (Gill), 19, *21*
doors (Schindler House), 81
Dreiser, Theodore, 29

E

Elks Club (Schindler), 8, *8*
Elliot House (Schindler), 29
Endo, Arato, *12*
Europe, construction in, 40
Experimental House am Horn (Gropius), 40 n. 3

F

fireplaces (Schindler House), *72–75*
Fireproof House (Wright), 40 n. 3
Five California Architects (McCoy), 43 n. 47
Floto, Julius, 12, *12*
Frampton, Kenneth, 40 n. 1
Friends of the Schindler House, 43 n. 47, 84, 85
Fujikura, Goichi, *12*
furniture (Schindler House), 25, 42 n. 24, 44, *45, 50, 52–54, 63–64, 70, 74–75*

G

Gale House (Wright), 40 n. 3
gardens and grounds (Schindler House), 36–37, 43 n. 47, *58, 61, 65,* 81, *82*
Gebhard, David, 38, 43 n. 47
Gibling, Dorothy, *24,* 25
Gibling, Edmund, *24,* 80
Gibling, Sophie, *24,* 80
Gibling, Sophie Pauline. *See* Schindler, Pauline
Giedion, Sigfried, 40 n. 1
Gill, Irving, 17–18, 42 n. 18; Dodge House, 19, *21;* La Jolla Woman's Club, *17*
Gold, Harriett, 84
Gropius, Walter: Bauhaus buildings, 33, 39; Experimental House am Horn, 40 n. 3; modernism of, 14; reputation of, 37; Schindler's influence on, 33; Sommerfeld House, 40 n. 3
guest studio (Schindler House), *23, 32, 68,* 81

H

Hardy, Thomas P., 13
Hitchcock, Henry-Russell, Jr., 40 n. 1, 42 n. 15; International Style exhibition, 38–40; *Modern Architecture,* 37
Hollein, Hans, 43 n. 47
Hollyhock House (Schindler and Wright), 14, 17, *17*

I

Imperial Hotel (Wright), 11, 12, 17
International Style exhibition, 38–40

J

Johnson, Philip, 37; International Style exhibition, 38–40

L

La Jolla Woman's Club (Gill), *17*
Larkin Administration Building (Wright), 9
Laurelwood Apartments (Schindler), 29
League of Nations Building (Schindler and Neutra), 28
Le Corbusier: Besnus House, 40 n. 3; Citrohan House, 40 n. 3; Monol House, 14; Ozenfant studio, 40 n. 3; reputation of, 37; Villa Savoye, 39, 40
light fixtures (Schindler House), *48, 74–75, 76*
The Little Review, 19
Loos, Adolf, 7–8; Steiner House, 19
Lovell, Leah, 27
Lovell, Phillip, 27
Lovell Beach House (Schindler), 28, 29, 43 n. 47
Lovell "Health" House (Neutra), 28
Lovell houses (Schindler), 27

M

MAK Center for Art and Architecture (Los Angeles), 85
March, Lionel, 43 n. 34, 43 n. 47
materials (Schindler House), 30–33, *30–32,* 36–37, 40, 81–82
Mayr and Mayer, 7
McCoy, Esther, 38, 84; *Five California Architects,* 43 n. 47
Mendelsohn, Erich, 43 n. 34
Mies van der Rohe, Ludwig: Barcelona Pavilion, 40 n. 3; brick country house, 40 n. 3; concrete country house, 33, *36,*

40 n. 3; modernism of, 14; reputation of, 37; Schindler on, 43 n. 46; Schindler's influence on, 33, 43 n. 34; Tugendhat House, 39, 40 n. 3
modern architecture, 40, 40 n. 1
Modern Architecture (Hitchcock), 37
modern house, first, 7, 39–40, 43 n. 47
Monol House (Le Corbusier), 14
Monolith Home (Schindler), *13,* 13–14, 19, 42 n. 15
Moser, Sylva, 26
Moser, Werner, 26

N
Neutra, Dion, 27, *28*
Neutra, Dione, 26, *26–27, 28*
Neutra, Frank, 26
Neutra, Richard, *28,* 43 n. 34; *Amerika,* 28; background of, 26; and Hitchcock, 37; and Johnson, 38; League of Nations Building, 28; Lovell "Health" House, 28; Schindler's friendship with, 7, 10, 26, 41 n. 15, 42 n. 30; Schindler's partnership with, 26–29; *Wie Baut Amerika?* 28
Niedermann, Doris, *27*
Noever, Peter, 85

O
Oliver House (Schindler), 29
Ottenheimer, Stern, and Reichert (Chicago), 8, 9, 10–11
Ozenfant studio (Le Corbusier), 40 n. 3

P
Pevsner, Nikolaus, 40 n. 1
plans (Schindler House), 19–21, *20–21,* 30, 33, *34–36,* 36–37, 40, 42 n. 31, 42 n. 33, 80–82
Popenoe House (Chace and Schindler), 25
Prairie Houses (Wright), 9
Pueblo Ribera Courts (Schindler and Chace), 25
pueblos (Taos), 9–10, *10*

R
Reed, John, 38
restoration (Schindler House), 43 n. 47, 84, 85
Rietveld, Gerrit, 14; Schröder House, 41 n. 3
Rodakiewicz House (Schindler), 29

roof (Schindler House), *56, 59*
Rowe, Colin, 40 n. 1
Russia, construction in, 40
Russian Revolution, 40

S
Sachs Apartments (Schindler), 29
Sarnitz, August, 43 n. 47
Scheyer, Galka, 28, *29*
Schindler, Mark, *24,* 25, 28, 29, 84
Schindler, Pauline ("Gibbie"; *née* Sophie Pauline Gibling), *24;* and the Chaces, 7, 18–19, 26, 42 n. 18; death of, 29, 84; health of, 26; leaves and returns to Schindler House, 28, 29; lifestyle of, 19; and Leah Lovell, 27; marriage to Schindler, 14, 16, 19, 25, 27, 28; names used by, 42–43 n. 32; personality of, 84; pregnancy and childbirth of, 24, 25; at Taliesin, 16, *16,* 84; and Wright, 42 n. 15. *See also* Schindler House
Schindler, Rudolph Michael, *24, 28;* background of, 7; Bethlehem Baptist Church, 29; Buena Shore Club clubhouse, 10–11, 41 n. 12; and the Chaces, 7, 18–19, 26, 42 n. 18; in charge of Wright's office, 11, 13, 41–42 n. 15; death of, 29; disappointment with Wright, 16–17; education and training of, 7; Elks Club, 8, *8;* Elliot House, 29; on family, 21; and Gill, 17–18; and Hitchcock, 37, 38; Hollyhock House, 14, *17;* immigrates to America, 8; and Johnson, 38; Laurelwood Apartments, 29; League of Nations Building, 28; lifestyle of, 19; and Loos, 7–8; Los Angeles practice of, 18, 19; Lovell Beach House, 28, 29, 43 n. 47; Lovell houses, 27; marriage to Pauline, 14, 16, 19, 25, 27, 28 (*see also* Schindler, Pauline); on Mies van der Rohe, 43 n. 46; Monolith Home, *13,* 13–14, 19, 42 n. 15; and Neutra, 7, 10, 26–29, 41 n. 15, 42 n. 30; Oliver House, 29; Popenoe House, 25; Pueblo Ribera Courts, 25; on pueblos vs. skyscrapers, 10; reputation/success of, 27, 29, 39, 43 n. 47; Rodakiewicz House, 29; Sachs Apartments, 29; at Taliesin, 14, 16, *16;* in Taos, 9–10, *10;* Tischler House, 29; Wolfe House, 29; and Wright, 8, 9, 10–11, 13, 41–42 n. 15, 41 n. 12; in

Yosemite National Park, 18, 19. *See also* Schindler House
Schindler Centennial (1987), 84, 85
Schindler court (Schindler House), *28, 47, 50, 54, 69, 71, 74–75*
Schindler House, 7, *39;* Banham on, 40; bathroom, *57;* Chace nursery, *58, 63, 66–67;* the Chaces leave, 26, 42 n. 29; Chace studios, *6,* 7, 24, 26, *26–27,* 28, *29, 39,* 42 n. 28, *58–67, 69, 77–79, 82;* construction, 18, *22,* 24–25, 30, *31–36, 32,* 40, 42 nn. 27–28, 81; as cooperative household, 25–26, 27, 81; design, 18–21, *20–21,* 24, 42 n. 24, 80–81; doors, 81; finances, 20, 24, 25, 26, 80; fireplaces, *72–75;* as first modern house, 7, 39–40, 43 n. 47; furniture, 25, 42 n. 24, 44, *45, 50, 52–54, 63–64, 70, 74–75;* gardens and grounds, 36–37, 43 n. 47, *58, 61, 65,* 81, *82;* goals for, 20–21, 42 n. 20; guest studio, *23, 32, 68,* 81; in history, 37–39, 43 n. 38, 43 nn. 46–47; influence of, 43 n. 34; light fixtures, *48, 74–75, 76;* materials, 30–33, *30–32,* 36–37, 40, 81–82; paint use, 25; plans, 19–21, *20–21,* 30, 33, *34–36,* 36–37, 40, 42 n. 31, 42 n. 33, 80–82; restoration, 43 n. 47, 84, 85; roof, *56, 59;* Schindler court, *28, 47, 50, 54, 69, 71, 74–75;* Schindler studios, *23, 30, 33, 39, 45–56, 59, 68, 70–76, 82;* site, 18–21, *19–23,* 42 n. 19, 81; sleeping baskets, *6,* 7, 30, 42 n. 28, *46, 48, 51, 55, 58, 60, 78–79,* 80; social life/artists at, 26, 27, 28–29; windows, 81; Wolfe House model, *52, 76;* Wright's influence on, 30
Schindler studios (Schindler House), *23, 30, 33, 39, 45–56, 59, 68, 70–76, 82*
Schröder House (Rietveld and Schröder), 41 n. 3
Sheine, Judith, 43 n. 47
site (Schindler House), 18–21, *19–23,* 42 n. 19, 81
slab-cast (slip-form) method, 25, 42 n. 27
slab-tilt method, 25, 32, 42 n. 27
sleeping baskets (Schindler House), *6,* 7, 30, 42 n. 28, *46, 48, 51, 55, 58, 60, 78–79,* 80
slip-form (slab-cast) method, 25, 42 n. 27
Smith, William E., *12,* 26
Sommerfeld House (Gropius), 40 n. 3

Steiner House (Loos), 19
Sweeney, Robert, 43 n. 47, 84

T
Taliesin (Wright), 9, *12, 15,* 16, 17, 30
textile-block houses, concrete, 40 n. 3
tilt-slab method, 18, 42 n. 18
Tischler House (Schindler), 29
T-Square, 38–39
Tsuchiura, Kameki, 26
Tsuchiura, Nobu, 26
Tugendhat House (Mies van der Rohe), 39,
    40 n. 3

U
Unity Temple (Wright), 9

V
Victorian houses, 9
Vienna, 7
Villa Savoye (Le Corbusier), 39, 40

W
Wasmuth, Ernst, 9
Wasmuth portfolio, 9, 16
Weston, Edward, 29
Wie Baut Amerika? (Neutra), 28
windows (Schindler House), 81
Winslow House (Wright), 40 n. 3
Wolfe House and model (Schindler), 29,
    52, 76
Workingman's Colony of Concrete Mono-
    lith Houses. *See* Monolith Home
World War I, 40
Wright, Frank Lloyd: American System-Built
    Houses, 40 n. 3; career and reputation
    of, 9; Chicago practice of, 11, *11,* 41
    n. 12; connection to nature in works of,
    16–17; Fireproof House, 40 n. 3; Gale
    House, 40 n. 3; and Gill, 42 n. 18; Holly-
    hock House, 14, 17, *17;* Imperial Hotel,
    11, 12, 17; influence on Schindler House,
    30; in Japan, 11, 13, 14, 41–42 n. 15;
    Larkin Administration Building, 9; Los
    Angeles practice of, 26; Prairie Houses,
    9; and Schindler, 8, 9, 10–11, 13, 41–42
    n. 15, 41 n. 12; Taliesin, 9, *12, 15,* 16, 17,
    30; Unity Temple, 9; Wasmuth portfolio
    of, 9, 16; Winslow House, 40 n. 3

Photograph Credits

References are to page numbers.

Architecture and Design Collection, University
Art Museum, University of California, Santa
Barbara, 5, 8, 10–13, 15, 16, 17 bottom, 20–21,
23 bottom, 30, 31 bottom, 34, 35 top, 39;
Courtesy of the Frank Lloyd Wright Archives,
12 top, 17 top; Friends of the Schindler
House, courtesy of the Schindler Family, 18,
22 top, 22 middle, 23 top, 24, 26, 31 top, 32,
33; Regula and Hans Fybel Collection, 27;
Drawing by Eulogio Guzman, copyright ©
Kathryn Smith, 35 bottom, 36; Courtesy of
Katherine Floto Loverud, 12 middle; Kathryn
Smith, 21; Courtesy of Kathryn Smith, 22
bottom, 28; UCLA Department of Geography
Air Photo Archives, 19; Peg Weiss/Valeska
Archives, 29.